The Basic Shelf
Cookbook

2011 EDITION

ISBN 1 894324 61 7

CPHA ✦ ACSP

CANADA'S PUBLIC HEALTH LEADER
LE LEADER CANADIEN EN SANTÉ PUBLIQUE

Canadian Public Health Association
404-1525 Carling Avenue, Ottawa, Ontario K1Z 8R9
Tel: 613-725-3769   Fax: 613-725-9826
publications@cpha.ca   publications.cpha.ca

About The Basic Shelf Cookbook

Welcome to *The Basic Shelf Cookbook!* This is a very special cookbook because all the recipes can be made from one list of low-cost, nutritious ingredients that make up what we call "the basic shelf". Most of these ingredients can be kept for a long time in your cupboard without refrigeration.

The Basic Shelf Cookbook was originally developed in the early 1990s by the City of York Health Unit and is designed for anyone living on a budget.

In this updated edition, the best recipes from the first edition of the cookbook were kept and a number of new recipes were added. The recipes are nutritious, tasty and are quick and easy to make. You do not need to be an expert cook or have a lot of expensive equipment to prepare these recipes. Using these recipes will help you save money and you will still be able to enjoy healthy, nutritious foods.

The Basic Shelf Cookbook also includes information about where to store food, a shopping guide to help you save money, meal planning ideas and tips for healthy eating.

Many thanks to everyone who helped to create *The Basic Shelf Cookbook*, including:
- The volunteers and staff of the City of York Health Unit who developed the first edition almost 20 years ago!
- The members of the 2011 Advisory Committee:
  - Debbie Boyd, Mi'kmaq Family & Children's Services
  - Fae Chen, York Region Community and Health Services
  - Lyndsay Davidson, Chatham Kent Public Health Unit
  - Janice McCue, Peterborough County-City Health Unit
  - Lucy Nobrega, Parmalat Canada
  - Tracy Pike, Trinity Conception Family Resource Centre
  - Elizabeth Smith, Nutrition Resource Centre, Ontario Public Health Association
  - Heather Thomas, Middlesex-London Health Unit
- Sue Mah of Nutrition Solutions Inc., our project consultant.

We also extend a very special thank you to Parmalat Canada which provided an unrestricted educational grant to support the development of this new edition.

Happy and healthy cooking!

Canadian Public Health Association
June 2011

Canadian Public Health Association

The Basic Shelf
Cookbook

Table of Contents

Snacks

Main Dishes

Meat and Poultry

Fish

Eggs and Cheese

Beans, Peas, Lentils and Tofu

Vegetables and Side Dishes

Desserts and Baked Treats

What is The Basic Shelf?

All the recipes in this cookbook can be made from one list of low cost, nutritious ingredients. This list of ingredients is called "the basic shelf". Most of these ingredients can be kept in your cupboard for a long time without refrigeration.

For most recipes in this cookbook, you will also need to buy a few fresh foods. The fresh foods you need are shown at the top of each recipe. Buy fresh ingredients in small amounts. They need to be kept in a refrigerator.

Keep these other tips in mind.

1. You do not have to buy all The Basic Shelf ingredients at once.

2. Buy only the amounts you know you have space to store.

3. Go to the bulk store or bulk section of your grocery store to buy: rice, grains, pasta, skim milk powder, baking ingredients, herbs and spices. That way, you can use up the ingredients before they go bad or lose their flavour.

4. Keep your Basic Shelf well stocked so you don't run out of important ingredients.

5. Be open. Try new foods like lentils, barley and tofu.

6. Choose brown rice and whole wheat pasta whenever you can because they have more fibre and nutrition than white rice and white pasta.

7. Buy the lower sodium or lower salt versions of The Basic Shelf ingredients that have an asterisk (*) beside them whenever possible.

8. Look for canned fruit that is packed in juice or juice from concentrate instead of packed in a light syrup.

9. Buy canned light tuna. It is cheaper and a better choice than canned albacore (white) tuna.

10. Use skim milk powder instead of fluid milk if you don't have a refrigerator and to save money.

Here is The Basic Shelf

Grain Products
- Rice and Grains
  - white rice
  - brown rice
  - barley
- Pasta (white and whole wheat)
  - elbow macaroni
  - spaghetti
  - lasagna
- Bread crumbs

Vegetables & Fruit
- Carrots
- Onions
- Potatoes
- Tomato paste
- Canned vegetables* (e.g., corn, tomatoes, mushrooms, peas, etc.)
- Canned vegetable soups* (e.g., tomato, mushroom, etc.)
- Canned fruit (e.g., peaches, pineapple, fruit cocktail, etc.)

Meat Alternatives
- Canned beans, peas and lentils (e.g., kidney beans, chick peas, brown lentils, etc.)
- Dried beans, peas and lentils (e.g., split peas, navy beans, etc.)
- Peanut butter
- Canned light tuna

Milk and Alternatives
- Skim milk powder (or use fluid milk in some recipes)

Fats and Oils
- Soft, non-hydrogenated margarine
- Vegetable oil (e.g., canola oil, soybean oil)

Baking Ingredients
- Flour
  - all purpose
  - whole wheat
- Sugar
  - white
  - brown
- Baking powder
- Baking soda
- Corn starch
- Raisins
- Rolled oats
- Vanilla extract (artificial)

Seasonings
- Salt
- Pepper
- Beef bouillon cubes* or Beef broth* or use the recipe for Homemade Beef Stock
- Chicken bouillon cubes* or Chicken broth* or use the recipe for Homemade Chicken Stock
- Dry mustard
- Garlic powder
- Ketchup*
- Soy sauce*
- Vinegar
- Worcestershire sauce
- Dried herbs (e.g., basil, Italian seasoning, oregano, thyme, etc.)
- Spices (e.g., paprika, cayenne, cinnamon, chili powder, etc.)

---

* Try to buy the lower sodium or lower salt versions of these foods and ingredients.

Where to Store Food

- Keep margarine, carrots and fluid milk in the refrigerator.

- Keep onions and potatoes in a cool, dark place. But store them away from each other because onions give off a gas that will spoil the potatoes.

- Store the other Basic Shelf ingredients in tightly sealed jars or plastic containers to keep out insects and other pests. Plastic containers and lids from margarine, yogurt and ice cream are good for storing rice, flour and cereal.

- Keep The Basic Shelf ingredients in a cool, clean dry place.

- Keep The Basic Shelf ingredients in a closet or on a shelf if you don't have enough space in the kitchen.

- Read the "expiry date" or "best before date" on canned foods and packages. Put the ones that will expire soon at the front of your shelf so you will know to use them first.

- Throw away any expired food or any food that you think may be spoiled.

- Write the date on the packages or containers of rice, pasta, dried beans, flour, rolled oats, raisins, herbs and spices when you buy them so you know how old the food is. Use the oldest foods first.

- Put any leftover canned foods (e.g., vegetables, fruit, tuna, beans, etc.) in a different container and cover it well. Keep it in the refrigerator and use it up within 2-3 days.

- Store leftovers in the refrigerator or freezer.

How Long Food Will Last

This chart shows how long the Basic Shelf ingredients and different leftovers will last.

Always check the best before date or expiry date of the food. Food that is spoiled may not look or smell differently. If you are not sure whether a food is spoiled or past its expiry date, then it is safer to throw it away.

Food	How long it will last
Grain Products	
• Rice – white rice	Several years
• Rice – brown rice	6-12 months
• Barley	6-12 months
• Pasta	2 years
• Bread crumbs	3 months
Vegetables and Fruit	
• Carrots (fresh)	Several weeks in the refrigerator
• Onions	2 months in a dark dry place *or* 3 weeks at room temperature
• Potatoes	2 months in a cool, dark, dry place *or* 1 week at room temperature
• Canned vegetables, soups, tomato paste, canned fruit	Check the expiry date
Meat Alternatives	
• Canned beans	Check the expiry date
• Dried beans	1 year
• Peanut butter	
– unopened	Check the expiry date
– opened	2 months
• Canned light tuna	Check the expiry date
Milk and Alternatives	
• Skim milk powder	
– unopened	1 year
– opened	1 month
• Fluid milk	Check the best before date

Food	How long it will last

Fats and Oils
- Soft, non-hydrogenated margarine
  - unopened — 8 months in the refrigerator
  - opened — 1 month in the refrigerator
- Vegetable oil — 1 year

Baking ingredients
- Flour
  - all purpose — 1 year
  - whole wheat — 3 months
- Sugar — Several years
- Baking powder, baking soda — 1 year
- Corn starch — 1½ years
- Raisins — 1 year
- Rolled oats — 6-10 months
- Vanilla extract — Several years

Seasonings
- Salt, pepper — Several years
- Beef or chicken bouillon cubes or broth — Check the expiry date
- Dried herbs, spices, garlic powder, dry mustard — 6 months (may keep longer but will lose flavour over time)
- Ketchup
  - unopened — 1 year on the shelf or cupboard
  - opened — 3 months on the shelf or cupboard
  - opened — 6 months in the refrigerator
- Vinegar — several years
- Soy sauce
  - unopened — 2 years
  - opened — 10-12 months
- Worcestershire sauce — 2 years

Leftovers or extra food
- Baked cakes, cookies — 4 months in the freezer
- Bread, buns — 1 month in the freezer
- Cooked casseroles — 2-3 days in the refrigerator / 3 months in the freezer
- Cooked meat — 3-4 days in the refrigerator / 2-3 months in the freezer
- Cooked poultry — 3-4 days in the refrigerator / 1-3 months in the freezer
- Soups, broth — 2-3 days in the refrigerator / 4 months in the freezer

Shopping Tips to Save Money

- **See what is on sale.** Look at grocery store flyers and newspaper ads to see what foods are on sale, and use this to plan your meals.

- **Make a grocery list.** Make a list of the foods and ingredients that you need to buy.

- **Bring a calculator.** Add up the cost of your groceries to help you stay on budget.

- **Get to know the food prices.** Write down or remember the regular prices of foods. This will help you figure out which stores have the best prices.

- **Avoid shopping when you are hungry.** When you are hungry, you may buy things you don't need.

- **Buy in season.** Vegetables and fruit are cheaper when they are in season.

- **Buy frozen or canned.** When fresh vegetables or fruit are too expensive, buy frozen or canned ones. They are just as nutritious. If using canned vegetables, try to buy the lower sodium or lower salt versions. Drain and rinse the vegetables under cold water first to wash away some of the salt and sodium.

- **Look high and low.** The less expensive items are usually on the higher or lower shelves.

- **Check the "best before" or expiry dates.** Choose foods with a far best before date or expiry date so you have more time to eat the food before it goes bad.

- **Check the "reduced" section.** Day old bread is good for making toast. Reduced vegetables are good for making soups. Ripe bananas are perfect for making muffins.

- **Compare brands.** No-name or store brands are still nutritious and are usually cheaper than the fancy brands.

- **Buy from the bulk bins.** Buy dried herbs, spices, rice, pasta, barley and flour from the bulk bin. Buy only the amount that you need to save money.

Shopping for Recipes

Using your recipes to make a shopping list is a great idea! But some of the store measurements are not the same as recipe measurements. This list will help you find the right amounts to buy.

Flour, 1 kg	gives you	9 cups (2 L + 250 mL) flour
Rice, 1 kg	gives you	6 cups (1.5 L) uncooked rice
Sugar, white, 1 kg	gives you	4½ cups (1 L + 125 mL) sugar
Brown sugar, 500 g	gives you	2½ cups (625 mL) brown sugar
1 lb (450 g) block cheese	gives you	4 cups (1 L) grated cheese
1 lb (450 g) margarine	gives you	2 cups (500 mL) margarine
1 lb (450 g) macaroni	gives you	4 cups (1 L) uncooked macaroni

What You Get

Sometimes it helps to know how much you will get from an ingredient.

Rice, uncooked ½ cup (125 mL)	gives you	1½ cups (375 mL) cooked rice
Pasta, uncooked ½ cup, (125 mL)	gives you	1 cup (250 mL) cooked pasta
Dried beans, raw 1 cup, (250 mL)	gives you	2 to 2½ cups (500 to 625 mL) cooked beans
Skim milk powder 1¼ cups, (300 mL)	gives you	4 cups (1 L) skim milk
Bananas 1-2 medium size bananas	gives you	1 cup mashed banana
Block cheese ¼ lb (125 g)	gives you	1 cup (250 mL) shredded cheese

What to Use If You Don't Have...

If you are missing an ingredient, you may have something on hand that you can use instead.

If you don't have...	Use...
Bread crumbs	Crushed cereal or cracker crumbs
Brown sugar, packed, 1 cup (250 mL)	White sugar, 1 cup (250 mL)
Buttermilk, 1 cup (250 mL)	Regular milk – use slightly less than 1 cup (250 mL) and add 1 tbsp (15 mL) lemon juice or white vinegar. Let stand for 5 minutes before using.
Corn starch, 1 tbsp (15 mL)	Flour, 2 tbsp (30 mL)
Dried herbs, ½ tsp (2 mL)	Fresh herbs, 1 tbsp (15 mL)
Dry mustard, 1 tsp (5 mL)	Prepared mustard, 1 tbsp (15 mL)
Garlic powder, tsp (½ mL)	Garlic, 1 clove
Homemade broth	Lower sodium broth in a can or carton, or bouillon cube
Homestyle Tomato Sauce with Herbs	Pasta sauce in a jar or can
Lemon juice, 1 tsp (5 mL)	Vinegar, ½ tsp (2 mL)
Tomato sauce, 2 cups (500 mL)	Tomato paste, ¾ cup (175 mL) + 1 cup (250 mL) water
Tomato soup, 1 can (10 oz)	Tomato sauce, 1 cup (250 mL) + ¼ cup (60 mL) water

How to Cook Dried Beans

Beans, split peas, chick peas and lentils all belong to the legume family. Legumes are plant foods which are high in protein, iron and fibre. They are low in fat. You can use legumes instead of meat to save money.

Canned beans are cooked and ready to use. Just drain and rinse them first.

Dried beans (except split peas and lentils) need to be soaked before cooking. Rinse beans and sort out any grit before you soak them.

To Soak Dried Beans

Put beans in a large pot. Add about 3 cups (750 mL) of water for each cup of beans. Now, follow one of the soaking methods below.

- **Overnight Soaking Method** – let soak for 8 to 12 hours or overnight. Drain.

OR

- **Quick Soaking Method** – Turn on stove to high heat. Heat beans to boiling. Turn down heat to low. Simmer for 2 to 3 minutes. Turn off heat, cover and let stand at least one hour. Drain.

To Cook Dried Beans

Turn on stove to high heat. Put rinsed and drained beans in a large pot. Add 2½ cups (675 mL) of water for each cup of beans. Heat to boiling. Turn down heat to low. Cover and simmer until tender.
Cooking times vary. Most beans take 1½ to 2 hours to cook.

How Much to Cook

Remember that beans will double when cooked.
Use this chart to help you figure out how much to cook.

If you need...	Use...
1 cup (250 mL) cooked beans	½ cup (125 mL) raw dried beans
2 cups (500 mL) cooked beans	1 cup (250 mL) raw dried beans
3 cups (750 mL) cooked beans	1½ cups (375 mL) raw dried beans
4 cups (1 L) cooked beans	2 cups (500 mL) raw dried beans

Meal Planning Tips to Save Money

- **Cook your own meals.** It is less expensive to cook your own meals than buy ready-to-eat, prepared meals. This cookbook has lots of great ideas, so try them all!

- **Use smaller amounts of meat, poultry and fish.** These are usually the most expensive foods. Mix these foods with less expensive foods such as bread, rice, pasta or potatoes.

- **Try to eat at least one meatless meal a week.** Make recipes that use low cost meat alternatives such as beans, eggs, tofu, peanut butter and canned fish.

- **Make a menu.** Plan ahead and write down what you would like to eat for breakfast, lunch, dinner and snacks for the week. Make a grocery list of the ingredients and foods you need.

- **Use leftovers.** Use leftover cooked chicken to make sandwiches. Use leftover rice or pasta to make a stir-fry or casserole. Add leftover vegetables to a soup or salad.

- **Make extras.** Make double of a recipe when the ingredients go on sale. Put the extras in the freezer to eat another time.

Basic Equipment List

Here is a list of all the equipment you will need to make the recipes in *The Basic Shelf Cookbook*. You do not have to buy all of this equipment at once. Buy a few things at a time to build your equipment list. Shop at discount stores or second hand stores to get the best prices.

Equipment/Utensil	Description
• Baking pans/baking dishes	– 13x9x2-inch (3.5 L) – 8x8x2-inch (2 L)
• Baking sheet	– 15 x 10 x ¾-inch
• Loaf pan	– 9x5x3-inch (2 L)
• Muffin tin	– 12 large cups
• Saucepans – small – medium	– 1 quart – 3 quart
• Large pots	– 8 quart – 12 or 16 quart
• Frypans	– 10-inch, non-stick – 8-inch, non-stick
• Casserole dish	– 2 Litre, covered
• Cutting boards	– 2 medium sized, plastic (buy 2 different colours if you can – use one for raw food only, and use the other for cooked food, fruits and vegetables)
• Knives	– 1 medium or large cook's knife – 1 paring knife
• Mixing bowls	– set of 4 plastic bowls, in a range of sizes from 1 qt (1 L) to 3 qt (3L)
• Measuring cup for liquids	– 2 cup (500 mL), glass or plastic

Equipment/Utensil	Description
• Measuring cups for dry ingredients	– 1 cup, ½ cup, ⅓ cup, ¼ cup, plastic
• Measuring spoons	– 1 tbsp, 1 tsp, ½ tsp, ¼ tsp
• Strainer (colander)	– hand held, plastic
• Grater	– hand held, metal
• Can opener	
• Vegetable peeler	
• Potato masher	
• Wooden spoon	
• Rubber spatula	
• Egg turner (or lifter)	
• Tongs	
• Soup ladle	
• Oven mitts	
• Whisk	

These next items are not needed, but are nice to have when you make some of the soup and dessert recipes:

• Handheld blender

• Pastry blender

Healthy Eating Tips

- **Eat regular meals.** Every day, try to eat breakfast, lunch, dinner and 2-3 snacks. Drink water when you are thirsty.

- **Eat a variety of foods every day.** This will help you get the different vitamins and minerals that you need. The nutrition information for each recipe tells you if the recipe is a good source or excellent source of different vitamins and minerals.

- **Eat balanced meals.** For a balanced breakfast, lunch or dinner, try to one food from at least 3 of the 4 food groups in Canada's Food Guide. For snacks, try to include one food from at least 2 of the food groups.

  The 4 food groups are:

  - **Vegetables and Fruit** – e.g., fresh, frozen or canned vegetables or fruit, 100% juice

  - **Grain Products** – e.g., bread, bagels, rice, pasta, cereal

  - **Milk and Alternatives** – e.g., milk, cheese, yogurt, fortified soy beverage

  - **Meat and Alternatives** – e.g., meat, poultry, beans, tofu, eggs, peanut butter, nuts, seeds

  For the Main Dishes recipes, there are serving ideas to help you put together a balanced meal.

  You can get a copy of Canada's Food Guide from your local public health department or on the Health Canada website at www.healthcanada.gc.ca

Basic Recipes

All Purpose Cheese Sauce

Try this cheese sauce over cooked vegetables like broccoli or cauliflower. Or pour it over a hot baked potato or freshly cooked pasta...delicious!

Basic Shelf +   **Cheese**
Yield   **1½ cups (375 mL)**

2 tbsp	margarine	30 mL
2 tbsp	flour	30 mL
¼ tsp	dry mustard	1 mL
1 cup	milk*	250 mL
1 cup	grated cheese	250 mL
	salt and pepper	

*   Use fluid milk or make enough from skim milk powder.

1. Turn on stove to medium heat. Melt margarine in a small saucepan. Add flour and mustard and mix well.

2. Add milk slowly, stirring all the time. Continue cooking and stirring until mixture is smooth and thickened. Lower heat and add grated cheese. Stir until cheese is melted. Add salt and pepper to taste.

Nutrition information per ¼ cup (60 mL)
• Good source of: vitamin B_{12}, vitamin D, calcium

Recipe from: *The Basic Shelf Cookbook*, First Edition 1994.

Baking Mix

This Baking Mix will keep in a cool, dry place for up to one month.

Basic Shelf + Yield	Nothing to add 6 cups (1.5 L)	
4 cups	all purpose flour	1 L
1½ cups	skim milk powder*	375 mL
3 tbsp	baking powder	45 mL
2 tbsp	sugar	30 mL
1½ tsp	salt	7 mL
¾ cup	vegetable oil	175 mL

* Use skim milk powder, not fluid milk in this recipe.

1. Put flour, skim milk powder, baking powder, sugar and salt into a large bowl. Mix well.

2. Add oil and stir until mixture looks crumbly. This will take about 5 to 7 minutes.

3. Put into a container with a tight fitting lid.

Use this **Baking Mix** to make **Oatmeal Banana Bread** - page 103.

Nutrition information per 1 cup (250 mL)
- Excellent source of: thiamine, riboflavin, niacin, folate, vitamin B_{12}, vitamin D, vitamin E, calcium, iron
- Good source of: vitamin A, magnesium, zinc
- A source of fibre

Recipe from: *The Basic Shelf Cookbook,* First Edition 1994.

Homestyle Tomato Sauce with Herbs

You can double this recipe. Store extra sauce in the refrigerator for up to one week, or in the freezer for up to six months.

Basic Shelf + Yield	Nothing to add about 4 cups (1 L)	
1 tbsp	vegetable oil	15 mL
1	chopped onion	1
1	can (28 oz/796 mL) tomatoes	1
3 tbsp	tomato paste	45 mL
2 tsp	sugar	10 mL
1 tsp	basil	5 mL
1 tsp	Italian seasoning	5 mL
1 tsp	dried oregano	5 mL
¼ tsp	garlic powder (or 2 garlic cloves minced)	1 mL
¼ tsp	pepper	1 mL
	salt	

1. Turn on stove to medium heat. Heat oil in medium saucepan. Add chopped onion and cook until soft, about 5 to 7 minutes.

2. Stir in tomatoes, tomato paste, sugar, salt, basil, Italian seasoning, oregano, garlic powder and pepper. Heat to boiling. Then turn down heat, cover and simmer for 40 minutes. Stir several times.

3. Add salt to taste.

Recipes in *The Basic Shelf Cookbook* which use **Homestyle Tomato Sauce with Herbs** are:
- Mini Pizzas – page 45
- Sloppy Joes – Page 52
- Italian-Style Meat Balls – page 53
- Tuna Rice Casserole – page 61
- Spinach Lasagna – page 67
- Carrot-Potato Pancakes – page 71
- Pasta with Vegetarian Sauce – page 73
- Cheesy Cauliflower – page 86
- Rice-Stuffed Green Peppers – page 95

Nutrition information per 1 cup (250 mL)
- Excellent source of: vitamin C, vitamin E
- Good source of: iron
- A source of fibre

Recipe from: *The Basic Shelf Cookbook*, First Edition 1994.

Homemade Chicken Stock

Bake your own chicken or buy one already cooked from the store.
Eat the meat and use the chicken bones to make this stock. You can also
use this recipe to make beef or vegetable stock.

Basic Shelf + **Yield**	**Chicken bones, Celery** **6-8 cups (1.5-2 L)**	
1 tbsp	vegetable oil	15 mL
2	large onions, chopped	2
3	carrots, chopped	3
4	celery stalks, chopped	4
	bones of one chicken	
	water	
1 tbsp	peppercorns	15 mL
5	sprigs of fresh thyme	5
	(or 1 tbsp /15 mL dried thyme)	
5	sprigs of fresh parsley	5
	(or 1 tbsp/15 mL dried parsley)	
1	bay leaf	1

1. Turn on stove to medium heat. Heat oil in a large pot. Add onions,
   carrots and celery. Cook until the vegetables start to get soft.

2. Add chicken bones. Fill the pot with enough cold water to cover the
   bones by about 2 to 3 inches (5 to 8 cm). Add peppercorns, thyme,
   parsley and bay leaf.

3. Heat stock on medium heat and bring to a gentle boil or simmer.
   Reduce heat to low or medium-low and continue to simmer for 1
   hour. Use a soup ladle to carefully skim off any scum.

4. Put a strainer or colander over an empty large pot or large glass bowl.
   When the stock has cooled, use a soup ladle to scoop the stock into
   the strainer. Throw away the herbs, bones and vegetables.

5. Cover the stock and put in the refrigerator overnight. The fat in the
   stock will form a hard layer on top. Use a spoon to scoop off this
   layer of fat and throw it away.

6. Keep the stock in the refrigerator for up to 3 days. Or freeze the stock
   in ½ cup (125 mL) containers for up to 4 months.

...continues

Homemade Chicken Stock

Recipes in *The Basic Shelf Cookbook* which use **Homemade Chicken Stock** are:
• Corn Chowder – page 26
• Chunky Vegetable Soup – page 27
• Minestrone Soup – page 29
• Split Pea, Bean and Barley Soup – page 30
• Lentil Soup – page 31
• Creamy Carrot Soup – page 32
• Potato Leek Soup – page 33
• Easy Chicken Stir-Fry – page 57

Nutrition information per 1 cup (250 mL) of chicken stock
• Good source of: niacin

Recipe adapted from: *Cook It Up! The Cookbook,* by London Community Resource Centre, 2010.

To make Homemade Beef Stock:
Follow the same steps for making chicken stock, but use beef bones instead of chicken bones.

To make Homemade Vegetable Stock:
Follow the same steps for making chicken stock, but do not use chicken.

Soups

Corn Chowder

This soup is a favourite for lunch, dinner, or anytime! If you have any leftover vegetables or leftover cooked meat, just add them to the soup too!

Basic Shelf+ Servings	Cream style corn 6 (each serving is 1 cup/250 mL)	
1 tbsp	margarine	15 mL
1	onion, chopped 1	
1½ cups	diced, raw potatoes	375 mL
2 cups	Homemade Chicken Stock*	500 mL
1½ cups	milk**	375 mL
1	can (19 oz/540 mL) cream style corn	1
	salt and pepper	

*   See recipe on page 23 or use store bought broth or bouillon cubes.
** Use fluid milk or make enough milk from skim milk powder.

1. Turn on stove to medium heat. Melt margarine in a large pot. Add chopped onion and cook until soft, about 5 to 7 minutes.

2. Add diced potatoes and Homemade Chicken Stock to the pot. Heat to boiling. Turn down the heat, cover and simmer until potatoes are almost tender, about 20 minutes.

3. Add milk and corn. Cook and stir mixture constantly over medium-low heat for about 4 to 5 minutes.

4. Add salt and pepper to taste.

Nutrition information per serving
• Excellent source of: folate
• Good source of: niacin, vitamin D
• A source of fibre

Recipe from: The *Basic Shelf Cookbook*, First Edition 1994.

Chunky Vegetable Soup

For a change, try canned chick peas or romano beans instead of kidney beans. Toss in any leftover carrots, green beans or frozen vegetables too.

Basic Shelf + Servings	Celery, Zucchini 10 (1 cup/250 mL)	
1 tsp	vegetable oil	5 mL
1	large onion, chopped	1
6 cups	Homemade Chicken Stock*	1.5 L
1	can (28 oz/796 mL) tomatoes	1
2 tbsp	dried parsley	30 mL
1 tbsp	dried basil	15 mL
1 tbsp	dried oregano	15 mL
4	carrots, chopped	4
4	celery stalks, chopped	4
2	potatoes, diced	2
1	zucchini, diced	1
1	can (19 oz/540 mL) kidney beans, drained and rinsed**	1
	salt and pepper	

*   See recipe on page 23 or use store bought broth or bouillon cubes.
** Or use about 2 cups (500 mL) cooked dried kidney beans. See page 14 for how to cook dried beans.

1. Turn on stove to medium heat. Heat oil in a large pot. Add chopped onion and cook until soft, about 5 minutes.

2. Add Homemade Chicken Stock, tomatoes, parsley, basil, oregano, carrots, celery and potato. Turn stove up to high heat, and heat to boiling. Lower heat and simmer until potatoes are almost tender, about 15 to 20 minutes.

3. Stir in diced zucchini and kidney beans. Add salt and pepper to taste. Simmer until zucchini is tender, about 15 minutes.

Nutrition information per serving
• Excellent source of: vitamin A, niacin, folate
• Good source of: thiamine, vitamin C, iron, magnesium
• Very high in fibre

Recipe from: *The Basic Shelf Cookbook*, First Edition 1994.

Tomato-Bean Soup with Cheddar

This quick and easy soup tastes great and is ready in about 10 minutes!

Basic Shelf +	**Stewed tomatoes, Beans in tomato sauce, Cheddar cheese**	
Servings	**4 (each serving is 1 cup/250 mL)**	
1	can (19 oz/540 mL) stewed tomatoes	1
1	can (14 oz/398 mL) beans in tomato sauce	1
1	cup water	250 mL
1 tsp	dried basil	5 mL
1 tsp	dried parsley	5 mL
½ cup	grated Cheddar cheese	125 mL
	green onions or chives (optional)	

1. Turn on stove to medium-high heat. Put tomatoes, beans, water, basil and parsley into a medium saucepan. Heat to boiling.

2. Turn down heat and simmer soup, uncovered, for 10 minutes. Stir several times.

3. Serve in bowls with grated cheese on top.

   Optional: Add chopped green onions or chives on top for extra flavour.

Nutrition information per serving
- Excellent source of: iron, zinc
- Good source of: thiamine, calcium, magnesium
- Very high in fibre

Recipe from: *The Basic Shelf Cookbook,* First Edition 1994.

Minestrone Soup

You can use any type of canned or dried beans in this recipe.

Basic Shelf + Servings	Cabbage 9 (each serving is 1 cup/250 mL)	
6 cups	Homemade Chicken Stock*	1.5 L
4 cups	chopped cabbage	1 L
3 cups	diced carrots	750 mL
2 cups	cooked navy beans** or 1 can (19 oz/540 mL) white kidney beans, drained and rinsed	500 mL
1	can (28 oz/796 mL) tomatoes	1
1/2 tsp	garlic powder	2 mL
	salt and pepper	
	Parmesan cheese, grated (optional)	

*   See recipe on page 23 or use store-bought chicken broth or bouillon cubes.
** To cook dried navy beans, see page 14.

1. Turn on stove to high heat. Put Homemade Chicken Stock in a large pot and heat to boiling.

2. Turn heat to low. Add chopped cabbage and diced carrots. Cover and simmer until vegetables are tender, about 20 minutes

3. Stir in beans, tomatoes and garlic powder. Add salt and pepper to taste. Cover and cook 5 minutes longer.

4. Serve in bowls with Parmesan cheese on top, if desired.

Nutrition information per serving
• Excellent source of: vitamin A, folate
• Good source of: thiamine, niacin, vitamin C, iron, magnesium
• High in fibre

Recipe from: *The Basic Shelf Cookbook*, First Edition 1994.

Split Pea, Bean and Barley Soup

What a great way to use up extra vegetables! Use extra dried green split peas if you don't have lima beans.

Basic Shelf +	**Celery**	
Servings	**6 (each serving is 1 cup/250 mL)**	
1 tbsp	vegetable oil	15 mL
2	onions, chopped	2
½ cup	dried green split peas	125 mL
¼ cup	dried lima beans	60 mL
¼ cup	barley	60 mL
5 cups	water or Homemade Chicken Stock*	1.25 L
1	bay leaf	1
1 tsp	celery seeds	5 mL
1	potato, diced	1
1	carrot, chopped	1
1	celery stalk, including leaves, chopped	1
1 tsp	dried basil	5 mL
½ tsp	dried thyme	2 mL
	salt and pepper	

* See recipe on page 23 or use store-bought chicken broth or bouillon cubes.

1. In a large pot, heat oil over medium heat. Add onions and cook, stirring until tender.

2. Rinse split peas and lima beans. Throw away any shriveled or discoloured ones. Add the split peas and lima beans to the pot. Add the barley, water (or Homemade Chicken Stock), bay leaf and celery seeds.

3. Bring to a boil. Reduce heat and simmer, covered for 1½ hours.

4. Add potato, carrot, celery, basil, thyme, salt and pepper. Simmer for 30 minutes or until vegetables are tender.

5. Remove bay leaf. If the soup is too thick, add water.

Nutrition information per serving
• Excellent source of: folate
• Good source of: vitamin A, thiamine, iron, magnesium
• High in fibre

Recipe from: *The Lighthearted Cookbook,* by Anne Lindsay, 1988. Recipe used with permission from Anne Lindsay. Copyright Anne Lindsay & Associates.

Lentil Soup

This is an easy and delicious soup.

Basic Shelf + Servings	Sweet potato, Celery 6 (each serving is about 1 cup/250 mL)	
2 cups	Homemade Chicken Stock or Homemade Vegetable Stock*	500 mL
1 cup	water	250 mL
1	onion, diced	1
1	sweet potato, peeled and diced	1
2	carrots, diced	2
2	celery stalks, diced	2
1	can (19 oz/540 mL) lentils, drained and rinsed**	1
½ tsp	cumin	2 mL

*   See recipe on page 23 or use store-bought broth or bouillon cubes.
** Or use about 2 cups (500 mL) cooked dried lentils. See page 14 for how to cook dried lentils.

1. Put all the ingredients into a medium pot. Bring to a boil.

2. Cover and simmer for 20 minutes or until the onions are soft.

3. Purée with a handheld blender or mash with a potato masher.

Nutrition information per serving
• Excellent source of: vitamin A, folate
• Good source of: thiamine, iron
• High in fibre

Recipe from: *The Ultimate Healthy Eating Plan…that still leaves room for chocolate*, by Liz Pearson and Marilyn Smith, 2002. Reprinted with permission from Whitecap Books Ltd.

Creamy Carrot Soup

A 2 pound bag of carrots will give you about 5-6 cups of sliced carrots.
Instead of carrots, you could make this soup with broccoli or cauliflower.

Basic Shelf +	**Nothing to Add**	
Servings	**6 (each serving is 1 cup/250 mL)**	
1 cup	Homemade Chicken Stock*	250 mL
4 cups	sliced carrots	1 L
¼ cup	margarine	60 mL
⅔ cup	finely chopped onion	150 mL
½ cup	flour	125 mL
3 cups	milk**	750 mL
	salt and pepper	

*   See recipe on page 23 or use store-bought broth or bouillon cubes.
** Use fluid milk or make enough with skim milk powder.

1. Turn on stove to medium heat. Put Homemade Chicken Stock into a medium saucepan. Add carrots and cook until soft. Add a little more water if necessary.

2. Mash the carrots with a vegetable masher. Scoop them out of the saucepan and set them aside.

3. Turn on stove to medium heat. Melt margarine in large saucepan. Add chopped onion and cook until soft, about 5 to 7 minutes.

4. Add flour and milk to onion. Cook and stir until mixture boils and is smooth and thick. Add mashed carrots and heat until hot. Add salt and pepper to taste.

Nutrition information per serving
- Excellent source of: vitamin A, riboflavin, vitamin D
- Good source of: thiamine, folate, vitamin B_{12}, calcium
- A source of fibre

Recipe from: *The Basic Shelf Cookbook,* First Edition 1994.

Potato Leek Soup

Leeks look like giant green onions. They add a nice flavour to this soup.

Basic Shelf + Servings	Leeks 12 (each serving is about 1 cup/250 mL)	
4	leeks	4
1 tbsp	vegetable oil	15 mL
2	large onions, chopped	1
4-5	medium sized potatoes, peeled and chopped	4-5
3	carrots, chopped	3
6 cups	Homemade Chicken Stock*	1.5 L
½ cup	plain yogurt**	125 mL
	salt and pepper	

*   See recipe on page 23 or use store-bought broth or bouillon cubes.
** For a thicker and creamier soup, use Balkan style yogurt.

1. Cut the base and the dark green parts of the leek. Throw away these parts.

2. Use only the light green and white parts of the leek. Slice these parts the leek into small strips. Put the leeks in a strainer (colander). Spread the layers apart and wash under cold water.

3. Turn on stove to medium-high heat. In a large pot, heat the oil and cook the onion until soft. Add leeks, potatoes, carrots, and Homemade Chicken Stock. Bring to boil. Reduce heat and simmer for about 15-20 minutes or until the vegetables are soft.

4. Remove from heat and let cool slightly. Use a hand held blender or potato masher to blend the soup until it is smooth.

5. Add salt and pepper to taste.

6. To reheat the soup, simmer over low heat. Pour into soup bowls and stir in about 1 tbsp (15 mL) yogurt in each bowl.

Nutrition information per serving
- Excellent source of: vitamin A
- Good source of: niacin
- A source of fibre

Recipe adapted from: Parmalat Canada, 2011

Notes

Salads

Coleslaw

This coleslaw will keep for one week in the refrigerator. After one day, it will become softer and more mellow tasting. For variety, add raisins, apples or chickpeas.

Basic Shelf + Servings	Cabbage 10 (each serving is 1 cup/250 mL)	
1	small cabbage, shredded	1
2 cups	grated carrots	500 mL
1	large onion, finely chopped	1
¼ cup	vegetable oil	60 mL
¼ cup	vinegar	60 mL
	salt and pepper	

1. Combine cabbage, carrots and onion in a large bowl. Set aside.

2. Mix oil and vinegar in a small bowl. Add salt and pepper to taste.

3. Pour oil and vinegar over cabbage mixture. Mix well.

4. Cover and refrigerate.

5. Just before serving, stir gently.

Nutrition information per serving
- Excellent source of: vitamin A
- Good source of: folate, vitamin C
- A source of fibre

Recipe from: *The Basic Shelf Cookbook,* First Edition 1994.

Mixed Bean Salad

This recipe makes a lot but it will keep a week in the refrigerator. You can use two cans of mixed beans instead of the kidney beans and chick peas.

Basic Shelf + Servings	Green Pepper 10 (each serving is 1 cup/250 mL)	
1	can (19 oz/540 mL) kidney beans*	1
1	can (19 oz/540 mL) chick peas*	1
1	can (14 oz/398 mL) yellow wax beans	1
1	can (14 oz/398 mL) green beans	1
1	medium onion, chopped	1
1	medium green pepper, chopped	1
⅔ cup	vinegar	150 mL
1/3 cup	vegetable oil	75 mL
¼ cup	sugar	60 mL
½ tsp	dried basil (optional)	2 mL
	salt and pepper	

*   Or use about 2 cups (500 mL) of cooked dried kidney beans and about 2 cups (500 mL) of cooked dried chick peas. See page 14 for how to cook dried beans.

1. Drain and rinse all of the canned beans. Put all of the beans, onion and green pepper into a large bowl.

2. Mix vinegar, oil, sugar and basil in a small bowl. Pour over bean mixture. Mix well.

3. Add salt and pepper to taste. Cover and refrigerate until cold.

4. Just before serving, stir gently.

Nutrition information per serving
- Excellent source of: folate
- Good source of: iron, magnesium
- High in fibre

Recipe from: *The Basic Shelf Cookbook*, First Edition 1994.

Garden Potato Salad

Red skinned potatoes look nice in this recipe. You can also use white or yellow potatoes.

Basic Shelf + Servings	Celery, Green Pepper 4 (each serving is 1 cup/250 mL)	
1	can (12 oz/341 mL) whole kernel corn niblets	1
2 cups	cooked, diced potato	500 mL
½ cup	finely chopped celery	125 mL
½ cup	finely chopped green pepper	125 mL
¼ cup	finely chopped onion	60 mL
3 tbsp	vegetable oil	45 mL
3 tbsp	vinegar	45 mL
¼ tsp	dry mustard	1 mL
¼ tsp	garlic powder	1 mL
	salt and pepper	
4	radishes, sliced (optional)	4

1. Drain and rinse the corn. Combine corn, potato, celery, green pepper and onion in a large bowl. Set aside.

2. Mix oil, vinegar, mustard and garlic powder in a small bowl. Pour over potato mixture. Mix well.

3. Add salt and pepper to taste. Cover and refrigerate.

4. Stir in radishes, if desired, just before serving.

Nutrition information per serving
- Excellent source of: folate, vitamin C
- Good source of: vitamin E, magnesium
- High in fibre

Recipe from: *The Basic Shelf Cookbook,* First Edition 1994.

Green Bean and Chick Pea Salad

Use fresh green beans when they are in season. In the winter, use a 19 oz (540 mL) can of cut green beans instead.

Basic Shelf + Servings	Green Beans 4 (each serving is about 1 cup/250 mL)	
1 lb	fresh green beans, trimmed, cut into 1-inch (2.5 cm) pieces	500 g
1	can (19 oz/540 mL) chickpeas, drained* and rinsed	1
¼ cup	finely chopped onion	60 mL
3 tbsp	vegetable oil	45 mL
3 tbsp	vinegar	45 mL
1 tsp	dried basil	5 mL
½ tsp	garlic powder	2 mL
	salt and pepper	

*   Or use about 2 cups (500 mL) of cooked dried chickpeas. See page 14 for how to cook dried beans.

1. Turn on stove to high heat. Half fill a medium pot with water and heat to boiling. Add green beans and cook until they are crisp-tender, about 5 minutes. Drain.

2. Put green beans, chickpeas and onion in a large bowl.

3. Mix oil, vinegar, basil and garlic powder in a small bowl. Add salt and pepper to taste. Pour over the green bean mixture. Mix well.

4. Cover and refrigerate until cold. Just before serving, stir gently.

Nutrition information per serving
*   Excellent source of: folate
*   Good source of: vitamin E, iron, magnesium, zinc
*   Very high in fibre

Recipe from: *The Basic Shelf Cookbook*, First Edition 1994.

Green Salad with All Purpose Salad Dressing

Mix and match! Use lettuce or spinach and any leftover raw vegetables that you have on hand. Add hard boiled eggs, tuna or nuts and seeds to make this a meal.

Basic Shelf + **Lettuce or Spinach, Leftover raw vegetables, Garlic, Lemon juice (or 1 fresh lemon)**

Servings 4-6

Salad

1	package (10 oz/284 g) salad mix or spinach OR 1 head of romaine lettuce	1
1½ cups	leftover raw vegetables, chopped (e.g., tomatoes, carrots, cucumber, peppers, etc.)	375 mL

All Purpose Salad Dressing

2 tbsp	vegetable oil	30 mL
1	clove garlic, minced (or 1/8 tsp /½ mL garlic powder)	1
2 tbsp	vinegar*	30 mL
1 tsp	sugar	5 mL
1 tsp	lemon juice	5 mL
½ tsp	dried oregano	2 mL
¼ tsp	pepper	1 mL

*   Use any type of vinegar you have on hand – white vinegar, cider vinegar, flavoured vinegar or Balsamic vinegar.

1. Wash and pat dry the lettuce leaves. Put the lettuce and vegetables in a large bowl.

2. Mix the oil, garlic, vinegar, sugar, lemon juice, oregano and pepper in a small bowl.

3. Just before eating, pour dressing over the salad and toss gently.

    Double this salad dressing for the **Pasta Salad** – page 41.

Nutrition information per serving
- Excellent source of: vitamin A, folate
- Good source of: vitamin C, vitamin E
- A source of fibre

Salad Dressing recipe adapted from: *Suppertime Survival*, by Lynn Roblin and Bev Callaghan, 2005.

Pasta Salad

For a change, try this salad with canned ham or canned chicken. In the summer, you can add sliced tomatoes for extra colour.

Basic Shelf +	**Cheddar or Mozzarella cheese, Green onion, Green pepper**	
Servings	**8**	
4 cups	cooked pasta (elbow macaroni or fusilli)	4 L
1	can (170 grams) canned light tuna, flaked and drained	1
1 cup	Cheddar cheese or Mozzarella cheese – grated or cubed	250 mL
¼ cup	thinly sliced green onions	60 mL
½ cup	green pepper, chopped	125 mL
1	carrot, chopped	1

All Purpose Salad Dressing (see recipe on page 40)

1. In a large bowl, combine pasta, tuna, cheese, green onion, green pepper and carrot.

2. Make double the recipe for All Purpose Salad Dressing. Just before eating, pour salad dressing over the pasta salad and toss gently.

Nutrition information per serving
- Excellent source of: vitamin A, niacin, folate, vitamin B_{12}
- Good source of: thiamine
- A source of fibre

Recipe adapted from: Parmalat Canada, 2011.

Notes

Snacks

Crispy Cheese Potatoes

Keep the potato skins on for extra fibre. Serve these right away while they are still crispy.

Basic Shelf +	**Cheese**	
Servings	**4**	
2	potatoes, scrubbed, washed and thinly sliced salt and pepper	2
½ cup	grated cheese	125 mL

1. Turn on oven to 400°F (200°C).

2. Place potato slices on a lightly greased baking sheet. Do not overlap slices. Sprinkle with salt and pepper.

3. Bake in oven 10 minutes, then turn the potatoes over. Bake another 10 to 15 minutes or until potatoes are tender.

4. Sprinkle cheese over potato slices. Return baking sheet to oven and bake until cheese is melted, about 1 to 2 minutes. Serve right away.

   Variation: Instead of cheese, you can sprinkle grated Parmesan cheese, paprika or chili powder. Add the seasonings to taste.

Nutrition information per serving
• A source of fibre

Recipe from: *The Basic Shelf Cookbook*, First Edition 1994.

Mini Pizzas

Everyone loves this snack! Look for whole wheat English Muffins for extra nutrition. Use other toppings such as canned pineapple, ham or leftover cooked meat.

Basic Shelf +	English muffins, Green pepper, Mushrooms, Cheese	
Servings	6 (each serving is 2 pieces)	
6	English muffins, cut in half	6
1½ cups	Homestyle Tomato Sauce with Herbs*	375 mL
¼ cup	finely chopped onion	60 mL
¼ cup	finely chopped green pepper	60 mL
¼ cup	sliced mushrooms (about 1 medium mushroom)	60 mL
1 cup	grated cheese	250 mL
	dried basil and dried oregano	
	salt and pepper	

* See recipe on page 22.

1. Turn on oven to 350°F (180°C).

2. Place English muffin halves on a baking sheet.

3. Spread Homestyle Tomato Sauce with Herbs on each muffin half. Sprinkle with basil, oregano, salt and pepper, to taste.

4. Put onion, green pepper and mushrooms on top of each muffin half. Sprinkle with cheese.

5. Bake until hot and bubbly, about 20 to 25 minutes.

Nutrition information per serving
• Excellent source of: folate
• Good source of: thiamine, niacin, calcium, iron
• A source of fibre

Recipe from: *The Basic Shelf Cookbook*, First Edition 1994.

Tuna Melt

Enjoy this for snack or a light lunch. For a change, use English muffins instead of bread. Add chopped green pepper to the tuna mixture for extra crunch if you like.

Basic Shelf + Servings	Cheese, Celery, Mayonnaise, Bread 6 (each serving is 1 slice of bread)	
1	can (170 g) light tuna, drained	1
1 cup	grated cheese	250 mL
½ cup	finely chopped celery	125 mL
¼ cup	finely chopped onion	60 mL
2 tbsp	mayonnaise	30 mL
	pepper	
6	slices bread	6

1. Turn on oven to 375°F (190° C).

2. Mix tuna, cheese, celery, onion and mayonnaise in a medium bowl. Add pepper to taste.

3. Put bread slices on a baking sheet.

4. Put equal amounts of tuna mixture on each bread slice and spread out evenly.

5. Bake in oven until cheese is melted, about 10 minutes.

6. Cut each slice of bread into four pieces. Serve right away.

Nutrition information per serving
- Excellent source of: niacin, vitamin B_{12}
- Good source of: thiamine, folate, calcium

Recipe adapted from: *The Basic Shelf Cookbook*, First Edition 1994

Seasoned Popcorn

Here are two different recipes. Put seasoned popcorn into a container with a tight fitting lid and keep it handy for when you want a snack.

Mexican Popcorn
You can use curry powder instead of chili powder.

Basic Shelf + Servings	Popcorn 8 (each serving is 1 cup/250 mL)	
8 cups	popped plain popcorn	2 L
3 tbsp	margarine, melted	45 mL
½ to 1 tsp	chili powder	2 to 5 mL
¼ to ½ tsp	garlic powder	1 to 2 mL
¼ to ½ tsp	dried thyme	1 to 2 mL
	salt and pepper	

1. Put popcorn into a large bowl. Pour melted margarine slowly over popcorn. Mix gently.

2. Add chili powder, garlic powder and thyme. Add salt and pepper to taste. Mix again.

Nutrition information per serving
• Source of: vitamin A, vitamin D, magnesium

Recipe from: *The Basic Shelf Cookbook,* First Edition 1994.

Parmesan & Herb Popcorn

Try other herbs, such as basil or thyme instead of oregano.

Basic Shelf + Servings	Popcorn, Parmesan cheese 8 (each serving is 1 cup/250 mL)	
8 cups	popped plain popcorn	2 L
3 tbsp	margarine, melted	45 mL
¼ cup	grated Parmesan cheese	60 mL
1 to 1½ tsp	dried oregano	5 to 7 mL
½ to 1 tsp	garlic powder	2 to 5 mL
	salt and pepper	

1. Put popcorn into a large bowl. Pour melted margarine slowly over popcorn. Mix gently.

2. Add Parmesan cheese, oregano and garlic powder. Add salt and pepper to taste. Mix again.

Nutrition information per serving
• Source of: vitamin A, vitamin B$_{12}$, vitamin D, magnesium

Recipe from: *The Basic Shelf Cookbook,* First Edition 1994.

Bean Dip

This dip is easy to make! Serve with raw veggies or pita breads cut into wedges.

Basic Shelf + Yield	Salsa, Garlic 8 cups	
1	can (19 oz/540 mL) black beans, drained and rinsed*	1
½ cup	salsa	125 mL
1	clove garlic, chopped (or 1/8 tsp or ½ mL garlic powder)	1
1 tsp	cumin	5 mL
pinch	pepper	pinch

* Or use about 2 cups (500 mL) of cooked dried black beans. See page 14 for how to cook dried beans.

1. In a bowl, combine beans, salsa, garlic, cumin and pepper.

2. Use a fork or potato masher to mash the ingredients. You can make a chunky dip, or mash it more to make a smoother dip.

Nutrition information per ¼ cup (60 mL)
• Good source of: folate
• A source of fibre

Recipe from: *You're the Chef*, by York Region Community and Health Services, 2009.

Notes

Main Dishes

Sloppy Joes

This is a quick and easy family favourite. Use ground chicken, ground turkey or ground pork for a change of flavour.

Basic Shelf + **Servings**	**Ground beef, Celery, Hamburger buns** **4**	
½ lb	ground beef	250 g
1	onion, finely chopped	1
1	celery stalk, finely chopped	1
1 cup	Homestyle Tomato Sauce with Herbs*	250 mL
½ tsp	Worcestershire sauce	2 mL
2 tbsp	corn starch	30 mL
2 tbsp	cold water	30 mL
2	hamburger buns, split, toasted	2
	salt and pepper	

*   See recipe on page 22.

1. Turn on stove to medium-high heat. Cook and stir beef, onion and celery in a large frypan. When meat is no longer pink, drain off fat.

2. Stir in Homestyle Tomato Sauce with Herbs and Worcestershire sauce.

3. Cook and stir until mixture boils. Turn heat to low. Simmer and stir, uncovered, 15 to 20 minutes or until vegetables are tender. Stir several times.

4. Combine corn starch and water in a small bowl. Stir into beef mixture. Cook and stir, until sauce has thickened, about 2 to 3 minutes. Add salt and pepper to taste.

5. Put the toasted bun halves on plates. Spoon Sloppy Joes mixture over buns. Serve right away.

Nutrition information per serving
- Excellent source of: niacin, vitamin B_{12}, zinc
- Good source of: thiamine, folate, iron
- A source of fibre

Recipe from: *The Basic Shelf Cookbook*, First Edition 1994.

Serving idea: *Add a slice of cheese to the sandwich, and serve with* **Green Salad with All Purpose Salad Dressing** *(page 40) or a piece of fruit.*

Italian-Style Meatballs

Instead of making ten meatballs, you could shape the meat into two hamburgers! Ground chicken, ground turkey or ground pork taste good in this recipe too!

Basic Shelf + **Servings**	**Ground beef, Eggs** **2**	
½ lb	ground beef	250 g
¼ cup	rolled oats	60 mL
1 tbsp	ketchup	15 mL
2 tbsp	finely chopped onion	30 mL
1	egg, beaten	1
½ tsp	Italian seasoning	2 mL
¼ tsp	pepper	1 mL
	salt	
2 tsp	vegetable oil	10 mL
¼ cup	water	60 mL
tsp	dry mustard	½ mL
2 tbsp	ketchup	30 mL

1. Put beef, oats, ketchup, onion, egg, Italian seasoning, pepper and salt to taste in a large bowl. Mix well.

2. Shape meat mixture into ten small balls.

3. Turn on stove to medium-high heat. Put oil in a small frypan. Add the meatballs. Cook and gently turn until browned on all sides. Turn heat to low. Cover and cook 10 to 15 minutes. Drain off fat.

4. Mix water mustard and ketchup in a small bowl. Pour over meatballs. Cover and cook 5 minutes longer.

Nutrition information per serving
- Excellent source of: riboflavin, niacin, vitamin B_{12}, zinc
- Good source of: thiamine, vitamin D, vitamin E, iron, magnesium
- A source of fibre

Recipe from: *The Basic Shelf Cookbook,* First Edition 1994.

Serving idea: *Serve meatballs on a whole wheat bun or with spaghetti and* ***Homestyle Tomato Sauce with Herbs*** *(page 22). Have some fresh veggies or fruit, and a glass of milk or fortified soy beverage.*

Spaghetti and Meat Sauce

This recipe tastes just as good with ground chicken, ground turkey or ground pork. Try grated carrots instead of zucchini next time too.

Basic Shelf + **Servings**	**Ground beef, Zucchini, Stewed tomatoes** **4**	
½ lb	ground beef	250 g
1	onion, finely chopped	1
3 cups	sliced zucchini (about 2 zucchini)	750 mL
1	can (19 oz/540 mL) stewed tomatoes	1
1 tsp	dried oregano	5 mL
	salt and pepper	
	hot cooked spaghetti	

1. Turn on stove to medium heat. Cook and stir ground beef and onion in a large frypan until the beef has browned. Drain off fat.

2. Add zucchini, tomatoes and oregano to the frypan. Heat to boiling. Lower heat, cover and simmer 25 to 30 minutes. Stir several times. Add salt and pepper to taste.

3. Serve sauce with hot cooked spaghetti.

Nutrition information per serving
- Excellent source of: thiamine, niacin, folate, vitamin B_{12}, iron, magnesium, zinc
- Good source of: riboflavin
- Very high in fibre

Recipe from: *The Basic Shelf Cookbook*, First Edition 1994.

Serving idea: *Enjoy with a glass of milk, or a glass of fortified soy beverage, or yogurt for dessert.*

Beef, Corn and Potato Casserole

Try frozen or other canned vegetables such as peas or carrots, or use leftover vegetables. Leave the skins on the potato for extra nutrition.

Basic Shelf + Servings	Ground beef 4	
4	medium potatoes, washed and eyes removed	4
1 lb	ground beef	500 g
1	onion, chopped	1
½ cup	milk*	125 mL
2 tbsp	margarine	30 mL
	salt and pepper	
1	can (12 oz/341 mL) whole kernel corn niblets, drained and rinsed	1
	paprika	

*   Use fluid milk or make enough milk from skim milk powder.

1.   Turn on stove to medium-high heat. Put potatoes in a large saucepan, cover with water and heat to boiling. Lower heat, cover saucepan and boil potatoes until tender.

2.   While potatoes are cooking, turn on another burner to medium heat. Cook and stir beef and onion in a large frypan until beef is browned. Drain off fat. Place meat mixture in an 8x8x2-inch (2 L) baking dish.

3.   Drain potatoes. Put potatoes back in saucepan. Use a potato masher and mash potatoes with milk and margarine. Add salt and pepper to taste. Set aside.

4.   Turn on oven to 350°F (180°C).

5.   Pour corn on top of meat. Spread potatoes over corn. Sprinkle lightly with paprika.

6.   Bake for about 30 minutes or until heated through.

Nutrition information per serving
• Excellent source of: niacin, folate, vitamin B$_{12}$, vitamin C, vitamin D, iron, magnesium, zinc
• Good source of: thiamine, riboflavin
• High in fibre

Recipe from: *The Basic Shelf Cookbook,* First Edition 1994.

Serving idea: *Have a small whole grain bun, bread or pita on the side. Serve with a glass of milk or a glass of fortified soy beverage.*

Chili Con Carne

This is a nice meal for a cold day.

Basic Shelf + Servings	Ground beef, Stewed tomatoes 4	
1lb	ground beef	500 g
1	large onion, chopped	1
2	cans (14 oz/398 mL) kidney beans, drained and rinsed*	2
1	can (19 oz/540 mL) stewed tomatoes	1
1 to 2 tsp	chili powder	5 to 10 mL
1 tsp	vinegar	5 mL
	salt	

*   Or use about 1½ cups (375 mL) cooked dried kidney beans.
    See page 14 for how to cook dried beans.

1. Turn on stove to medium heat. Cook and stir ground beef in a
    medium saucepan until the beef is no longer pink. Drain off fat.

2. Stir in onion, beans, tomatoes, chili powder and vinegar. Add salt to
    taste. Heat to boiling.

3. Turn heat down to low. Simmer, uncovered, for 35 to 40 minutes.
    Stir chili several times while it cooks.

Nutrition information per serving
• Excellent source of: thiamine, niacin, folate, vitamin B_{12}, iron,
  magnesium, zinc
• Good source of: riboflavin
• Very high in fibre

Recipe from: *The Basic Shelf Cookbook*, First Edition 1994.

Serving idea: Dip a piece of bread or bun in the chili. Serve with **Green Salad with All Purpose Salad Dressing** *(page 40)* or **Honey Glazed Carrots** *(page 87). For your drink, have a glass of milk or a glass of fortified soy beverage.*

Easy Chicken Stir-Fry

This stir-fry tastes great with any type of vegetables – fresh, frozen or canned. Use different soft, medium and firm vegetables for variety. You can also use boneless chicken thighs, lean pork or your favourite lean meat.

Basic Shelf +	Chicken, Garlic, Ginger Fresh vegetables (or canned or frozen ones)	
Servings	4-6	
⅔ cup	Homemade Chicken Stock or Homemade Vegetable Stock*	150 mL
2 tbsp	soy sauce	30 mL
1 tsp	sugar	5 mL
2 tsp	corn starch	10 mL
¾ lb	boneless chicken breast or thighs	350 g
4 cups	mixture of fresh vegetables**	1 L
2 tbsp	vegetable oil	30 mL
1	onion, cut in thin wedges	1
6	cloves garlic, minced (or ¾ tsp or 3 mL garlic powder)	6
2 tsp	minced ginger (or ¼ tsp or 1 mL ginger powder)	10 mL

*   See recipe on page 23 or use store-bought broth or bouillon cubes.
** Firm vegetables are: carrots, broccoli, cauliflower, celery, green beans
     Medium vegetables are: peppers, zucchini, snow peas, mushrooms, green peas
     Soft vegetables are: bean sprouts, spinach

1. Place the stock, soy sauce, sugar and corn starch in a small bowl. Whisk together and set this sauce aside.

2. Cut the chicken into thin strips.

3. Using a clean cutting board, slice the vegetables into bite sized pieces.

4. Heat just half of the oil (1 tbsp or 15 mL) in a large frying pan. Add the chicken to the pan and stir-fry until the chicken is no longer pink inside. Remove from pan and put on a clean plate.

...continues

Easy Chicken Stir-Fry, continued

5. Heat the rest of the oil (1 tbsp or 15 mL) in pan. Add the onion, garlic and ginger stir-fry for one minute.

6. Add the other vegetables, starting with the firm ones, then add the medium and soft vegetables 1-2 minute later.

7. Add the chicken and stir-fry for one more minute to heat through.

8. Add the sauce to the same pan, stirring constantly until clear.

Nutrition information per serving
• Excellent source of: vitamin A, niacin, vitamin C
• Good source of: vitamin E, magnesium
• A source of fibre

Recipe from: *Cooking Up Some Fun!*, by York Region Community and Health Services, 2006.

Serving idea: *Serve on cooked rice, pasta or noodles. Enjoy yogurt for dessert.*

Stove-Top Barbecued Chicken

Serve with rice or pasta to soak up this delicious barbecue sauce.

Basic Shelf + Servings	Chicken Legs 4	
1 tsp	vegetable oil	5 mL
½ cup	chopped onion	125 mL
½ cup	ketchup	125 mL
½ cup	water	125 mL
2 tbsp	vinegar	30 mL
2 tbsp	brown sugar	30 mL
1 ½ tsp	Worcestershire sauce	7 mL
1 tsp	dried parsley	5 mL
½ to 1 tsp	chili powder	2 to 5 mL
4	chicken legs, skin removed and fat trimmed off	4
1 tbsp	corn starch	15 mL
1 tbsp	cold water	15 mL

1. Turn on stove to medium-high heat. Heat oil in a large frypan. Add onion and cook until soft, about 5 minutes.

2. Stir in ketchup, water, vinegar, brown sugar, Worcestershire sauce, parsley and chili powder and. Heat sauce until it boils.

3. Add chicken. Spoon sauce over chicken. Turn heat to low, cover and simmer 30 minutes. Turn chicken over and cook another 15 minutes. Remove chicken and put on a clean plate. Leave sauce in the frypan.

4. Turn up heat to medium. Combine corn starch and water in a small bowl. Stir into sauce. Cook and stir until mixture boils and thickens. To serve, spoon sauce over chicken.

Nutrition information per serving
- Excellent source of: riboflavin, niacin, zinc
- Good source of: vitamin B$_{12}$

Recipe from: *The Basic Shelf Cookbook,* First Edition 1994.

Serving idea: *Serve with* **Rice Primavera** *(page 94) or cooked pasta with some vegetables. Add a glass of milk or fortified soy beverage.*

Herb Baked Chicken

Don't worry if you have chicken left over. It tastes delicious cold and is perfect for lunch.

Basic Shelf + Servings	Chicken Legs, Parmesan Cheese 4	
4	chicken legs, skin removed and fat trimmed off	4
½ cup	milk*	125 mL
⅓ cup	bread crumbs	75 mL
⅓ cup	Parmesan cheese	75 mL
1 tbsp	dried parsley	15 mL
1 tsp	Italian seasoning	5 mL
¼ tsp	pepper	1 mL

*   Use fluid milk or make enough milk from skim milk powder.

1. Place chicken in a medium bowl. Pour milk over chicken and let soak for 5 minutes. Turn over and let soak for another 10 minutes. Drain chicken. Throw away the milk.

2. Turn on oven to 375°F (190°C). Stir bread crumbs, cheese, parsley, Italian seasoning and pepper together in a medium bowl.

3. Dip chicken pieces, one at a time, into bread crumb mixture. Be sure each piece of chicken is coated all over.

4. Lightly grease a baking pan and place the chicken pieces in the pan. Bake about 45 minutes or until chicken is well cooked.

Nutrition information per serving
- Excellent source of: niacin, vitamin B_{12}, zinc
- Good source of: thiamine, riboflavin

Recipe from: *The Basic Shelf Cookbook*, First Edition 1994.

Serving idea: *Serve with **Rice, Onion and Mushroom Pilaf** (page 97) or cooked pasta. Add a vegetable side dish or fruit. Have a glass of milk or fortified soy beverage.*

Tuna Rice Casserole

Serve with **Homestyle Tomato Sauce With Herbs** (page 22) if you like. Instead of canned tuna, you can use canned chicken or canned ham. You can use frozen corn or frozen peas instead of canned corn.

Basic Shelf + Servings	Cheddar cheese 4	
2 cups	water	500 mL
1 cup	rice	250 mL
2 tbsp	margarine	30 mL
½ cup	chopped onion	125 mL
3 tbsp	flour	45 mL
1½ cup	milk*	375 mL
1 tsp	Worcestershire sauce	5 mL
1	can (170 g) light tuna, drained and flaked	1
1	can (12 oz/341 mL) whole kernel corn niblets, drained and rinsed	1
	salt and pepper	
½ cup	grated Cheddar cheese	125 mL

*   Use fluid milk or make enough milk from skim milk powder.

1.   Turn on stove to high heat. Put water and rice in a medium saucepan. Heat to boiling, Turn heat to low, cover, and simmer until rice is tender. This will take about 20 minutes and all the water will be absorbed.

2.   Turn on oven to 375°F (190°C).

3.   While rice is cooking, turn on another burner to medium heat. Melt margarine in a large saucepan. Add onion and cook until soft, about 3 to 5 minutes. Stir in flour. Pour milk in slowly, stirring all the time. Add Worcestershire sauce. Cook and stir until mixture boils and thickens.

4.   Add cooked rice, tuna and corn to sauce. Mix well. Add salt and pepper to taste.

...continued

Tuna Rice Casserole, continued

5. Lightly grease an 8x8x2-inch (2 L) baking pan. Spread mixture into pan. Sprinkle with cheese.

6. Bake in oven for 20 to 25 minutes or until hot.

Nutrition information per serving
- Excellent source of: riboflavin, niacin, folate, vitamin B_{12}, vitamin D
- Good source of: vitamin A, thiamine, calcium, magnesium, zinc
- A source of fibre

Recipe from: *The Basic Shelf Cookbook,* First Edition 1994.

Serving idea: *Serve with a piece of fruit for dessert.*

Tuna Broccoli Bake

A fast and easy meal!

Basic Shelf + Servings	Broccoli, Cheese 4	
1	large bunch broccoli, cut into bite-sized pieces	1
1	can (10 oz/284 mL) condensed mushroom soup	1
½ cup	milk*	125 mL
1	can (170 g) light tuna, drained, flaked	1
1 cup	grated cheese, divided	250 mL

*   Use fluid milk or make enough milk from skim milk powder.

1. Turn on stove to high heat. Half fill a medium pot with water and heat to boiling. Add broccoli and cook until crisptender, about 3 to 5 minutes. Drain.

2. Turn on oven to 350°F (180°C).

3. Lightly grease an 8x8x2-inch (2 L) casserole dish. Arrange the broccoli on the bottom of the dish.

4. Mix soup, milk, tuna and ½ cup (125 mL) of the cheese in a medium bowl. Spoon over broccoli.

5. Sprinkle remaining ½ cup (125 mL) cheese on top. Cover.

6. Bake casserole until hot and bubbly, about 20 to 30 minutes.

Nutrition information per serving
- Excellent source of: vitamin A, riboflavin, niacin, folate, vitamin B$_{12}$, vitamin C, calcium
- Good source of: vitamin E, iron, magnesium, zinc
- A source of fibre

Recipe from: *The Basic Shelf Cookbook,* First Edition 1994.

Serving idea: *Serve on rice, pasta or toast.*

Easy Seafood Burgers

This recipe makes 4 small patties and tastes just as delicious with canned salmon.

Basic Shelf + **Servings**	**Celery, Relish, Eggs, Green onions** **4**	
1	can (170 g) tuna or can (7½ oz/213 g) salmon, drained (if using salmon, remove skin and large bones)	1
¼ cup	celery, finely chopped	60 mL
2 tbsp	relish	30 mL
2	eggs, lightly beaten	2
½ cup	bread crumbs	125 mL
2	green onions, chopped	2
	salt and pepper to taste	

1. In a large mixing bowl, combine all ingredients.

2. Shape into 4 patties.

3. Turn on stove to medium-high heat. In a non-stick pan, cook patties until both sides are golden brown - about 3 minutes per side.

Nutrition information per serving
- Excellent source of: niacin, vitamin B$_{12}$
- Good source of: thiamine, folate

Recipe from: *Eating for energy without deprivation,* by Patricia Chuey and Diana Steele, 2004.

Serving idea: *Serve on whole wheat toast. Add a salad and a glass or milk or fortified soy beverage.*

Zippy Cheese Bake

For extra fibre and colour, add a handful of leftover chopped vegetables such as broccoli or green pepper.

Basic Shelf + Servings	Bread, Cheese, Eggs 4	
2 cups	cubed bread	500 mL
1 cup	grated cheese	250 mL
2	eggs	2
2 cups	milk*	500 mL
2 tbsp	vegetable oil	30 mL
tsp	pepper	½ mL
	salt	
	paprika	

* Use fluid milk or make enough milk from skim milk powder.

1. Turn on oven to 350°F (180°C).

2. Lightly grease an 8x8x2-inch (2L) baking pan. Spread about half the bread cubes over the bottom of the baking pan. Sprinkle the grated cheese over the bread cubes. Arrange the rest of the bread cubes over the cheese.

3. Mix eggs, milk, vegetable oil and pepper in a medium bowl. Add salt to taste. Pour egg mixture over bread. Let stand 10 minutes.

4. Sprinkle paprika lightly over the top.

5. Place baking pan in a larger pan that has been half filled with hot water. Put both pans into the oven together.

6. Bake in oven about 40 to 45 minutes. To see if the casserole is cooked, put a small knife into the middle of it. If it comes out clean, the casserole is done.

Nutrition information per serving
- Excellent source of: riboflavin, vitamin B_{12}, vitamin D, calcium
- Good source of: vitamin A, thiamine, niacin, folate, vitamin E, zinc

Recipe from: *The Basic Shelf Cookbook*, First Edition 1994.

Serving idea: *Serve with **Sweet Potato Baked Fries** (page 90).*

Quick Macaroni and Cheese

A warm and satisfying "comfort food".

Basic Shelf +	Cheddar cheese	
Servings	4	
1 cup	elbow macaroni, uncooked	250 mL
2 tbsp	margarine	30 mL
2 tbsp	flour	30 mL
¼ tsp	dry mustard	1 mL
1 cup	milk*	250 mL
1 cup	grated Cheddar cheese	250 mL
	salt and pepper	

*   Use fluid milk or make enough milk from skim milk powder.

1.   Turn on stove to high heat. Add about 4 cups (1 L) of water to a large saucepan and heat until it boils. Add the elbow macaroni. Starting from the time the water boils again, cook for about 10 minutes, stirring several times. Drain and set aside.

2.   Meanwhile, melt margarine in a medium saucepan. Stir in flour and mustard. Add milk slowly, stirring all the time. Cook and stir until mixture boils and thickens.

3.   Turn stove to low heat. Add cheese and stir until cheese is melted and sauce is smooth.

4.   Add drained macaroni. Mix gently. Stir over low heat until mixture is hot. Add salt and pepper to taste.

Nutrition information per serving
• Excellent source of: folate, vitamin D, calcium
• Good source of: vitamin A, thiamine, riboflavin, niacin, vitamin B$_{12}$, zinc

Recipe from: *The Basic Shelf Cookbook,* First Edition 1994.

Serving idea: *Toss in any leftover chicken, ground beef, ham or tuna. Have some carrots, beans, peas or other vegetable.*

Spinach Lasagna

This recipe is a crowd pleaser. You could bake two and freeze one for another day.

Basic Shelf +	Spinach, Cottage cheese, Cheddar or Mozzarella cheese	
Servings	**6**	
9	lasagna noodles	9
2	packages (10 oz/284 g) fresh spinach	2
2 cups	Homestyle Tomato Sauce with Herbs*	500 mL
1	can (5½ oz/156 mL) tomato paste	1
1 tbsp	dried parsley	15 mL
1 tsp	dried oregano	5 mL
1 tsp	salt	5 mL
½ tsp	pepper	2 mL
1	container (500 g) cottage cheese	1
1½ cups	grated Cheddar or Mozzarella cheese	375 mL

*   See recipe on page 22.

1. Cook lasagna noodles according to package directions. Make sure they are still slightly firm. Drain and set aside.

2. Meanwhile, cut the coarse stems off the spinach. Wash and dry the leaves. Put the trimmed spinach in a medium saucepan. Add about ¼ cup (60 mL) of hot water. Turn on stove to high heat. Cover and cook for 2 to 3 minutes. Rinse spinach with cold water. Put in a strainer to drain.

3. Turn on stove to medium-high heat. Combine Homestyle Tomato Sauce with Herbs, tomato paste, parsley, oregano, salt and pepper in a large saucepan. Cook and stir until mixture boils. Turn heat to low. Simmer, uncovered, for 10 minutes.

4. Turn on oven to 350°F (180°C). Spread a thin layer of sauce on the bottom of a 13x9x2-inch (3.5 L) baking pan.

...continues

Spinach Lasagna, continued

5. Arrange 3 lasagna noodles over the sauce. Spread with ⅓ of the sauce, ⅓ of the cottage cheese, ⅓ of the spinach and ⅓ of the grated cheese.

6. Repeat Step 5 two more times.

7. Bake lasagna for about 30 to 40 minutes. Let stand 10 minutes before serving.

Nutrition information per serving
- Excellent source of: vitamin A, thiamine, riboflavin, niacin, folate, vitamin B_{12}, vitamin E, calcium, iron, magnesium, zinc
- Good source of: vitamin C
- Very high in fibre

Recipe from: *The Basic Shelf Cookbook*, First Edition 1994.

Serving idea: Serve with carrot sticks or **Green Salad with All Purpose Salad Dressing** (page 40).

Vegetable Frittata

A perfect recipe if you have a leftover cooked potato. This tastes good even without the potato!

Basic Shelf+ Servings	Eggs, Green pepper, Mushrooms, Cheese 2	
2	eggs	2
1 tsp	margarine	5 mL
1 tbsp	chopped onion	15 mL
1 tbsp	chopped green pepper	15 mL
1 tbsp	chopped mushrooms (about 1 mushroom)	15 mL
½ cup	thinly sliced cooked potato	125 mL
2 tbsp	grated cheese	30 mL

1. Beat eggs in a small bowl. Set aside.

2. Turn on stove to medium heat. Melt margarine in a small frypan. Add onion, green pepper and mushrooms and cook until soft, about 5 to 7 minutes. Drain off any liquid.

3. Next, pour eggs over vegetables in frypan. Turn heat to low, cover and cook until eggs are cooked but still soft in the middle.

4. Arrange potato slices on top of eggs. Sprinkle with cheese. Cover and cook a few minutes longer until cheese is melted. Serve right away.

Nutrition information per serving
- Excellent source of: vitamin B_{12}
- Good source of: riboflavin, folate, vitamin D

Recipe from: *The Basic Shelf Cookbook,* First Edition 1994.

Serving idea: *Serve with bread or toast. Have yogurt with fruit for dessert.*

Crispy Potato and Carrot Casserole

Use Cheddar, Swiss, Mozzarella or your favourite cheese.

Basic Shelf + Servings	Eggs, Cheese 6	
6	potatoes, grated	6
3	carrots, grated	3
1	onion, grated	1
1 cup	skim milk powder*	250 mL
¼ cup	rolled oats	60 mL
2	eggs, beaten	2
3 tbsp	vegetable oil	45 mL
1 tsp	garlic powder	5 mL
½ tsp	salt	2 mL
1 tsp	pepper	5 mL
1 cup	grated cheese	250 mL

* Do not use fluid milk.

1. Turn on oven to 350°F (180°C). Mix grated potatoes, carrots and onion in a large bowl.

2. Stir in skim milk powder, rolled oats, eggs, oil, garlic powder, salt and pepper.

3. Lightly grease a 13x9x2-inch (3.5 L) baking pan. Spread mixture evenly into the pan.

4. Bake about 30 to 40 minutes, or until potatoes are done.

5. Sprinkle with cheese. Return to oven for a few minutes to melt cheese.

Nutrition information per serving
- Excellent source of: vitamin A, thiamine, riboflavin, niacin, vitamin B_{12}, vitamin D, calcium, magnesium, zinc
- Good source of: folate, vitamin C, vitamin E, iron
- High in fibre

Recipe from: *The Basic Shelf Cookbook,* First Edition 1994.

Serving idea: *Serve with a slice of bread or a small bun.*

Carrot-Potato Pancakes

If you have any of these delicious pancakes left over, put them in the refrigerator and reheat later.

Basic Shelf + Servings	Eggs 4	
4	eggs	4
2 cups	finely grated carrot	500 mL
2 cups	finely grated potato	500 mL
1 tbsp	finely grated onion	15 mL
2 tbsp	flour	30 mL
½ tsp	salt	2 mL
½ tsp	pepper	2 mL
½ tsp	baking powder	2 mL
	vegetable oil	
	Homestyle Tomato Sauce with Herbs* (optional)	

* See page 22 for recipe.

1. Beat eggs in a large bowl. Stir in carrot, potato, onion, flour, salt, pepper and baking powder. Mix well.

2. Turn on stove to medium-high heat. Heat a small amount of oil in a large frypan.

3. Pour about ¼ cup (60 mL) carrot-potato mixture into frypan. Spread out into a pancake. Repeat until there are as many pancakes in the frypan as it will hold.

4. Fry pancakes until bottoms are crisp and brown. Turn and cook the other sides until vegetables are tender. You will need about 4 to 5 minutes per side. As the pancakes are done, put them on a plate and keep them warm.

5. Add a little more oil to pan, as needed. Continue making pancakes until all the carrot-potato mixture is used.

6. Serve pancakes with hot Homestyle Tomato Sauce with Herbs (page 22) or sour cream if you like.

Nutrition information per serving
- Excellent source of: vitamin A, vitamin B_{12}
- Good source of: thiamine, riboflavin, folate, vitamin E
- A source of fibre

Recipe from: *The Basic Shelf Cookbook*, First Edition 1994.

Serving idea: *Serve with a slice of bread or small bun. Drink a glass of glass of milk or a glass of fortified soy beverage.*

Vegetable Fried Rice

You could use 2 cups of leftover cooked rice for this recipe instead of cooking the rice from scratch.

Basic Shelf + Servings	Celery, Green Pepper and Eggs 4	
2 cups	water	500 mL
1 cup	rice	250 mL
1 tsp	vegetable oil	5 mL
½ cup	thinly sliced celery	125 mL
½ cup	thinly sliced onion	125 mL
½ cup	thinly sliced carrots	125 mL
½ cup	thinly sliced green pepper	125 mL
4	eggs, beaten	4
1-2 tbsp	soy sauce	15-30mL
	salt and pepper	

1. Turn on stove to high heat. Combine water and rice in medium saucepan. Heat to boiling. Turn down heat, cover and simmer until rice is tender. This will take about 20 minutes and all the water will be absorbed. When the rice is cooked, set it aside.

2. Then turn on stove to medium-high heat. Heat oil in large frypan. Add celery, onion, carrots and green pepper and stir-fry until vegetables are crisp-tender, about 6 to 8 minutes.

3. Add eggs to vegetable mixture. Cook and stir to scramble eggs. While eggs are still runny, stir in cooked rice and soy sauce. Continue to cook and stir just until the mixture is hot. Add salt and pepper to taste.

Nutrition information per serving
• Excellent source of: vitamin A, vitamin B_{12}
• Good source of: riboflavin, folate, vitamin E
• A source of fibre

Recipe from: *The Basic Shelf Cookbook*, First Edition 1994.

Serving idea: *Serve with a glass of glass of milk or a glass of fortified soy beverage.*

Pasta with Vegetarian Sauce

This is a good meatless meal. You could serve the sauce on rice instead of pasta too.

Basic Shelf+ Servings	Celery, Zucchini, Tomato Sauce 10 (3/4 cup/175 mL)	
1 tsp	vegetable oil	5 mL
½ cup	finely chopped onion	125 mL
½ cup	finely chopped carrots	125 mL
½ cup	thinly sliced celery	125 mL
1½ cups	sliced zucchini	375 mL
4 cups	Homestyle Tomato Sauce with Herbs*	1 L
1	can (19 oz/540 mL) lentils, drained and rinsed**	1
1	can (10 oz/284 mL) mushrooms, drained and rinsed	1
1 tsp	dried oregano	5 mL
1 tsp	Italian seasoning	5 mL
¼ tsp	garlic powder	1 mL
	salt and pepper	

*   See recipe on page 22.
**   Or use 2 cups (500 mL) of cooked dried lentils. See page 14 for how to cook dried lentils.

1. Turn on stove to medium-high heat. Heat oil in a large pot. Add onion, carrots, celery and zucchini. Cook and stir until vegetables are slightly soft, about 8 to 10 minutes.

2. Stir in Homestyle Tomato Sauce With Herbs, lentils, mushrooms, oregano, Italian seasoning and garlic powder. Heat to boiling. Turn down heat to low, cover and simmer until vegetables are tender, about 30 to 40 minutes. Add salt and pepper to taste.

3. Serve with hot cooked pasta or rice.

Nutrition information per serving (with 1 cup/250 mL cooked pasta):
• Excellent source of: thiamine, niacin, folate, iron
• Good source of: vitamin A, magnesium, zinc
• Very high in fibre

Recipe from: *The Basic Shelf Cookbook,* First Edition 1994.

Serving idea: *Add a salad or some veggies. Finish with yogurt for dessert.*

Rice with Creole Kidney Beans

Use more or less chili powder depending on how spicy you like your food.

Basic Shelf + Servings	Celery, Green Pepper 6	
1 tsp	vegetable oil	5 mL
1	large onion, chopped	1
2	celery stalks, chopped	2
1 cup	chopped carrots	250 mL
1	green pepper, chopped	1
½ tsp	garlic powder	2 mL
1	can (5½ oz/156 mL) tomato paste	1
1½ cups	water	375 mL
1 to 2 tsp	chili powder 5 to 10 mL	
1 tsp	dried oregano	5 mL
1 tsp	vinegar	5 mL
½ tsp	dry mustard	2 mL
2	cans (19 oz/540 mL) kidney beans, drained and rinsed* salt and pepper	2
1½ cups	rice	375 mL
3 cups	water	750 mL

* Or use 4 cups (1 L) of cooked dried kidney beans. See page 14 for how to cook dried beans.

1. Turn on stove to medium heat. Heat oil in a large saucepan. Add onion and cook until soft, about 5 minutes.

2. Add celery, carrots, green pepper and garlic powder. Cook and stir over medium heat until vegetables are tender, about 15 minutes.

3. Add tomato paste, water, chili powder, oregano, vinegar, mustard and kidney beans to the vegetables. Cook and stir until mixture boils. Turn heat to low. Add salt and pepper to taste.

...continues

Rice with Creole Kidney Beans, continued

4. Cover and simmer for about 40 minutes. Stir several times. Add more water if mixture seems too thick.

5. Meanwhile, put rice and 3 cups (750 mL) water into a medium saucepan. Turn stove to high heat and heat until the water boils. Turn heat to low, cover, and simmer until rice is tender. This will take about 20 minutes and all the water will be absorbed.

6. Serve the bean mixture over hot cooked rice.

Nutrition information per serving
- Excellent source of: vitamin A, folate, iron, magnesium
- Good source of: thiamine, niacin, vitamin C, vitamin E, zinc
- Very high in fibre

Recipe from: *The Basic Shelf Cookbook*, First Edition 1994.

Serving idea: *Serve with a glass of milk or a glass of fortified soy beverage or yogurt.*

Pasta and Beans

This is a hearty and delicious recipe for lunch or dinner.

Basic Shelf + Servings	Celery 4	
1 cup	elbow macaroni	250 mL
1	can (28 oz/796 mL) tomatoes	1
2 cups	diced carrots	500 mL
3	celery stalks, chopped	3
1	large onion, chopped	1
1½ tsp	dried oregano	7 mL
1½ tsp	dried parsley	7 mL
¼ tsp	garlic powder	1 mL
1	can (14 oz/398 mL) kidney beans, drained and rinsed	1
	salt and pepper	

1. Turn on stove to high heat. Half fill a medium saucepan with water and heat to boiling. Add elbow macaroni. Cook about 10 minutes, starting from the time the water boils again, stirring several times. Drain and set aside.

2. While macaroni is cooking, turn on another burner on the stove to medium-high heat. Put tomatoes, carrots, celery, onion, oregano, parsley and garlic powder into a large saucepan. Cook and stir until mixture boils.

3. Turn heat to low, cover, and simmer until vegetables are crisp-tender, about 20 minutes. Stir mixture several times while cooking.

43 Add cooked macaroni and kidney beans to tomato mixture. Add salt and pepper to taste. Simmer for 10 minutes.

Nutrition information per serving
- Excellent source of: vitamin A, thiamine, niacin, folate, vitamin C, iron, magnesium
- Good source of: riboflavin, vitamin E, zinc
- Very high in fibre

Recipe from: *The Basic Shelf Cookbook*, First Edition 1994.

Serving idea: *Enjoy with a glass of milk or a glass of fortified soy beverage.*

Chickpea Burgers

This is like a falafel except it is not deep fried. The tahini sauce adds extra flavour but is optional. If you don't have tahini, you can use peanut butter.

Basic Shelf +	**Egg, Green onion, Pita bread** **(To make the tahini sauce: Yogurt, Tahini,** **Lemon juice)**
Servings	**4**

Chickpea Burgers

1	can (19 oz/540 mL) chickpeas, drained and rinsed*	1
4	green onions, trimmed and sliced	4
1	egg	1
2 tbsp	all purpose flour	30 mL
1 tbsp	chopped fresh oregano or ½ tsp (2 mL) dried oregano	15 mL
½ tsp	ground cumin	2 mL
¼ tsp	salt	1 mL
2 tbsp	vegetable oil	30 mL
2	pita breads (6½ inches)	2

*   Or use 2 cups (500 mL) of cooked dried chickpeas instead. See page 14 for how to cook dried chickpeas.

Tahini Sauce (optional)

½ cup	plain yogurt	125 mL
2 tbsp	tahini (or peanut butter)	30 mL
1 tbsp	lemon juice	15 mL
⅓ cup	chopped, flat-leaf parsley or about 2 tsp (10 mL) dried parsley	75 mL
¼ tsp	salt	1 mL

**   Tahini is smooth, thick paste made from ground sesame seeds. It is available in the Middle Eastern section or near the other nut butters at large supermarkets.

...continues

Chickpea Burgers, continued

Chickpea Burgers
1. Place chickpeas, green onions, egg, flour, oregano, cumin and salt in big bowl. Use a potato masher or fork to mash the ingredients. The mixture will be moist and should hold together when pressed. Form into 4 patties.

2. Heat oil in a large nonstick pan over medium-high heat. Add patties and cook until golden and beginning to crisp, about 4 to 5 minutes. Carefully flip and cook until golden brown, 2 to 4 minutes more.

3. Cut the pita breads in half and warm them up if you like. Put one chickpea patty in each pita half. Serve with Tahini sauce (optional).

Tahini Sauce
1. Combine yogurt, tahini, lemon juice, parsley and salt in a medium bowl. Mix and serve with the chickpea burgers.

Nutrition information per serving (without tahini sauce)
- Excellent source of: folate
- Good source of: thiamine, niacin, vitamin E, iron, magnesium, zinc
- High in fibre

Recipe from *EatingWell* and *www.EatingWell.com*, 2006.

Serving idea: *Add lettuce, cucumbers, tomatoes or other vegetables in the pita. Enjoy with a glass of milk or a glass of fortified soy beverage or yogurt.*

Speedy Lentil and Bean Casserole

This recipe only takes about 10 minutes to make – that's speedy!

Basic Shelf + Servings	Celery, Mozzarella cheese 6-8	
1 tbsp	vegetable oil	15 mL
1	large onion, chopped	1
3	celery stalks, chopped	3
1	can (540 mL/19 oz) kidney beans, drained and rinsed*	1
2 cups	cooked lentils**)	500 mL
1	can (28 oz/796 mL) canned tomatoes, drained	1
1 tsp	dried thyme	5 mL
	pepper	
1½ cups	grated Mozzarella cheese	375 mL

*   Or use 2 cups (500 mL) cooked dried kidney beans. See page 14 for how to cook dried kidney beans.

** See page 14 for how to cook dried lentils. Or use 1 can (540 mL/19 oz) canned lentils, drained and rinsed instead.

1. Turn on the broiler in the oven.

2. In the saucepan, heat the oil over medium heat. Cook the onion and celery until softened.

3. Add the beans, lentils, tomatoes, thyme and pepper to taste. Bring mixture to a simmer with stirring. Break up the tomatoes using the back of a spoon.

4. Transfer mixture to the casserole dish for serving. Sprinkle the cheese over the surface and put under the broiler. Watch it carefully and remove when the cheese has just melted.

Nutrition information per serving
• Excellent source of: niacin, folate, iron, magnesium, zinc
• Good source of: thiamine, vitamin C, vitamin E, calcium
• Very high in fibre

Recipe adapted from: *Community Food Advisor Resource Binder*, by Nutrition Resource Centre, 2008.

*Serving idea: Have with a slice of whole wheat bread or bun. Add **Green Salad with All Purpose Dressing** (page 40) or other vegetables or a piece of fruit.*

Teriyaki Tofu

Tofu is made from soybeans and is an economical meat alternative. It picks up any flavour you add to it. Use soy sauce if you don't have teriyaki sauce.

Basic Shelf + Servings	Tofu, Teriyaki cooking sauce 4	
1	package (454 g) of medium-firm tofu	1
2 tbsp	vegetable oil	30 mL
⅓ cup	teriyaki cooking sauce	75 mL

1. Carefully cut the block of tofu in half lengthwise. Then cut each half diagonally into 2 large triangle-shaped pieces.

2. Turn on stove to medium-high heat. Heat oil in a frying pan. Add tofu and cook until lightly brown and crispy, about 5 minutes per side.

3. Pour teriyaki sauce over the cooked tofu.

Nutrition information per serving
• Good source of: folate, calcium, magnesium

Recipe from: *Eating for energy without deprivation,* by Patricia Chuey and Diana Steele, 2004.

Serving idea: *Serve with* **Vegetable Fried Rice** *(page 72) or* **Rice, Onion and Mushroom Pilaf** *(page 97). Enjoy with a glass of milk or fortified soy beverage.*

Tofu and Vegetable Rice

This is a good recipe if you're trying tofu for the first time.

Basic Shelf +	Tofu, Celery, Green onions, Frozen green peas, Fresh garlic, Fresh ginger	
Servings	**6**	
1	package (350 g) of medium-firm tofu	1
2½ cups	Homemade Chicken Stock*	625 mL
1¼ cups	rice, uncooked	300 mL
½ cup	chopped celery	125 mL
½ cup	chopped green onions	125 mL
⅔ cup	frozen green peas, thawed	160 mL
2 tsp	soy sauce	10 mL

Marinade

2 tsp	vegetable oil	10 mL
1½ tsp	minced garlic (about 2 garlic cloves)	7 mL
1 tsp	minced ginger	5 mL
¼ tsp	pepper	1 mL
2 tbsp	soy sauce	30 mL

*   See recipe on page 23 or use store bought broth or bouillon cubes.

1. In a bowl, mix the marinade ingredients together. Cut the tofu into cubes and add to the marinade. Let the tofu sit in the marinade for at least 20 minutes.

2. In a medium pot, add Homemade Chicken Stock and rice. Simmer for 10 minutes. Add celery and cook until the liquid has absorbed.

3. Add tofu and marinade to the cooked rice. Add green onions, green peas and remaining soy sauce. Heat through. Garnish with chopped green onions if you wish.

Nutrition information per serving
- Good source of: thiamine, niacin, folate, magnesium, zinc
- A source of fibre

Recipe from: Soy for Life, 2011 www.soyforlife.ca

Serving idea: *Have with a cup of milk or fortified soy beverage.*

Notes

Vegetables and Side Dishes

Stir-Fried Veggies

Use different vegetables when they are a good buy. For example, use green pepper, zucchini, or green beans in the summer instead of onion, carrots, or celery.

Basic Shelf + **Servings**	**Broccoli, Celery** **4**	
1½ cups	small pieces of broccoli	375 mL
1 tsp	vegetable oil	5 mL
1 cup	thinly sliced onion	250 mL
1 cup	thinly sliced carrot	250 mL
1 cup	thinly sliced celery	250 mL
2 tsp	corn starch	10 mL
3 tbsp	cold water	45 mL
1-2 tbsp	soy sauce	15-30 mL
	pepper	

1. Turn on stove to high heat. Half fill a medium saucepan with water and heat to boiling. Cook broccoli in boiling water for 3 minutes. Drain. Put broccoli in cold water and drain again.

2. Turn on stove to medium-high heat. Heat oil in a large frypan. Add broccoli, onion, carrots and celery. Stir-fry until vegetables are crisp-tender, about 6 to 8 minutes.

3. Mix corn starch, water and soy sauce in a small bowl. Stir into vegetables. Cook and stir until sauce boils and thickens. Add pepper to taste. Serve right away.

Nutrition information per serving
- Excellent source of: vitamin A, folate
- Good source of: vitamin C
- A source of fibre

Recipe from: *The Basic Shelf Cookbook*, First Edition 1994.

Broccoli and Mushroom Gratin

This recipe is easy to make and bake!

Basic Shelf + Servings	Broccoli 4 large	
1	large bunch broccoli, cut into bite-sized pieces	1
2 tbsp	margarine	30 mL
⅓ cup	finely chopped onion	75 mL
2 tbsp	flour	30 mL
1 cup	milk*	250 mL
1 tsp	Worcestershire sauce salt and pepper	5 mL
1	can (10 oz/284 mL) sliced mushrooms, drained and rinsed	1
2 tbsp	bread crumbs	30 mL

*   Use fluid milk or make enough from skim milk powder.

1. Turn on oven to 350°F (180°C).

2. Turn on stove to high heat. Half fill a large pot with water and heat to boiling. Add broccoli and cook until crisptender, about 3 to 5 minutes. Drain and set aside.

3. While broccoli is cooking, turn on another burner to medium heat. Melt margarine in a large saucepan. Add onion and cook until soft, about 3 to 5 minutes.

4. Stir in flour. Pour milk in slowly, stirring all the time. Cook and stir until mixture boils and thickens. Add Worcestershire sauce. Add salt and pepper to taste. Stir in broccoli and mushrooms.

5. Put broccoli mixture into an 8x8x2-inch (2 L) baking pan. Bake in oven 15 to 20 minutes or until hot.

6. Sprinkle with bread crumbs and bake 5 minutes longer.

Nutrition information per serving
• Excellent source of: vitamin A, folate, vitamin C, vitamin D
• Good source of: thiamine, riboflavin, vitamin E, magnesium
• High in fibre

Recipe from: *The Basic Shelf Cookbook*, First Edition 1994.

Cheesy Cauliflower

Serve this vegetable side dish with any of the main dishes.

Basic Shelf + Servings	Cauliflower, Cheese 4	
1	small head cauliflower, cut into bite sized pieces, (about 4 cups/1 L)	1
1½ cups	Homestyle Tomato Sauce With Herbs*	375 mL
2 tbsp	bread crumbs	30 mL
2 tbsp	grated cheese	30 mL

*   See recipe on page 22.

1. Turn on oven to 350°F (180°C).

2. Turn on stove to high heat. Half fill a medium pot with water and heat to boiling, Add cauliflower and cook until crisptender, about 3 to 5 minutes. Drain and set aside.

3. Put cauliflower in an 8x8x2-inch (2 L) baking dish. Pour Homestyle Tomato Sauce With Herbs over the cauliflower.

4. Combine bread crumbs and cheese in a small bowl. Sprinkle over tomato sauce.

5. Cover and bake in oven about 20 to 25 minutes or until hot.

Nutrition information per serving
- Excellent source of: folate, vitamin C
- Source of: thiamine, riboflavin, niacin, vitamin E, calcium, iron, magnesium, zinc
- A source of fibre

Recipe from: *The Basic Shelf Cookbook*, First Edition 1994.

Honey Glazed Carrots

This recipe takes about 5 minutes. Use baby carrots or chopped regular carrots. If you don't have honey, try brown sugar.

Basic Shelf +	**Nothing to add**	
Servings	**4**	
2 cups	baby carrots	500 mL
1 tbsp	margarine	15 mL
1 tbsp	honey or brown sugar	15 mL

1. Steam carrots until they are tender-crisp. (If you do not have a steamer, put the carrots in a medium saucepan and add just enough water to cover the carrots. Boil until the carrots are tender-crisp.)

2. Drain. Add the margarine and honey or brown sugar. Heat until bubbly.

Nutrition information per serving
• Excellent source of: vitamin A

Recipe from: *The Ultimate Healthy Eating Plan...that still leaves room for chocolate*, by Liz Pearson and Marilyn Smith, 2002. Reprinted with permission from Whitecap Books Ltd.

Scalloped Potatoes with Cheese and Herbs

Your friends will be asking for this recipe!

Basic Shelf+ Servings	Cheese 4	
1 tbsp	margarine	15 mL
½ cup	finely chopped onion	125 mL
¼ tsp	garlic powder	1 mL
1½ cups	milk*	375 mL
½ tsp	salt	2 mL
¼ tsp	dried basil	1 mL
¼ tsp	dried oregano	1 mL
¼ tsp	pepper	1 mL
2 tbsp	bread crumbs	30 mL
2 tbsp	grated cheese	30 mL
3	medium potatoes, thinly sliced	3
¼ cup	grated cheese	60 mL

*   Use fluid milk or make enough milk from skim milk powder.

1.   Turn on stove to medium heat. Melt margarine in a small frypan. Add onion and garlic powder. Cook until onion is soft, about 3 to 5 minutes. Set aside.

2.   Meanwhile, turn on stove to medium heat. Heat milk, salt, basil, oregano and pepper in a large saucepan. Set aside.

3.   Combine bread crumbs and 2 tbsp (30 mL) cheese in a small bowl. Set aside.

43   Turn on oven to 350°F (180°C). Lightly grease an 8x8x2-inch (2 L) casserole dish.

5.   Arrange one third of the potatoes on the bottom of the dish. Put half of the onion mixture on top of the potatoes. Sprinkle with half of the bread crumb mixture. Next put in half the remaining potatoes. Spread the rest of the onions and bread crumb mixture over the second potato layer. Put the last third of the potatoes on top.

...continues

Scalloped Potatoes with Cheese and Herbs, continued

6. Pour hot milk mixture into casserole. Sprinkle with ¼ cup (60 mL) cheese.

7. Cover and bake until potatoes are tender, about 50 to 60 minutes. Let stand 10 minutes before serving.

Nutrition information per serving
- Excellent source of: vitamin D
- Good source of: thiamine, riboflavin, niacin, vitamin B_{12}, vitamin C, calcium, magnesium
- A source of fibre

Recipe from: *The Basic Shelf Cookbook*, First Edition 1994.

Sweet Potato Baked Fries

Sweet potatoes are more nutritious than white potatoes. The kids will love these too!

Basic Shelf + **Servings**	**Sweet potatoes** **4**	
4	sweet potatoes	4
2 tbsp	vegetable oil	30 mL
	salt and pepper	
	Parmesan cheese (optional)	

1. Heat oven to 450°F (230°C).

2. Peel sweet potatoes. Rinse and dry well. Cut into wedges or small sticks.

3. Put sweet potatoes in a bowl and coat well with vegetable oil.

4. Arrange potatoes on a baking sheet. Bake 15 minutes. Turn the fries over and bake for another 15 minutes until slightly crispy.

5. Season to taste with salt and pepper and Parmesan cheese if you wish.

Nutrition information per serving
- Excellent source of: vitamin A
- Good source of: vitamin E
- A source of fibre

Recipe from: *Colour It Up Resource Binder*, by Nutrition Resource Centre 2007.

Butternut Squash with Brown Sugar and Cinnamon

Butternut squash has a nice creamy texture when it is cooked.
This recipe works with acorn squash too.

Basic Shelf + Servings	Butternut squash 6	
2 lb	butternut squash	900 g
2 tsp	margarine	10 mL
2 tsp	brown sugar	20 mL
1 tsp	ground cinnamon	5 mL

1. Using a large knife cut the squash into quarters. Scoop out the seeds.

2. Place the butternut squash into a microwave-safe casserole dish.* Dot with margarine and the brown sugar. Microwave on high for 10 to 15 minutes or until soft.

3. When cooked through, scoop out the flesh into a bowl. Mash with a fork or potato masher. Sprinkle with cinnamon.

*   If you do not have a microwave, you can bake the squash.

    Heat oven to 350 F (180 C). Line a baking sheet with aluminium foil. Cut squash in half, lightly oil, place cut side down, and bake for 50 to 60 minutes or until squash is soft. Scoop out the flesh into a bowl. Mash and mix in the margarine, brown sugar and cinnamon.

Nutrition information per serving
• Excellent source of: vitamin A, vitamin C, vitamin E, magnesium
• Good source of: thiamine, folate
• High in fibre

Recipe from: *The Ultimate Healthy Eating Plan...that still leaves room for chocolate*, by Liz Pearson and Marilyn Smith, 2002. Reprinted with permission from Whitecap Books Ltd.

Skillet Zucchini with Chopped Tomatoes

This is great recipe for the summer and fall when tomatoes and zucchini are in season.

Basic Shelf + Servings	Zucchini, Tomatoes 4	
1 tsp	margarine	5 mL
2	small onions, chopped	2 mL
4	small zucchini, thinly sliced	4
2	medium tomatoes, chopped	2
	pepper	

1. In a large nonstick skillet, melt margarine over medium heat.

2. Add onions and cook, stirring until softened.

3. Add zucchini and cook for 2 minutes.

4. Add tomatoes and cook for 3 to 5 minutes or until zucchini is tender-crisp.

5. Season to taste with pepper.

Nutrition information per serving
- Good source of: vitamin C
- A source of fibre

Recipe from: The Lighthearted Cookbook, by Anne Lindsay, 1988. Recipe used with permission from Anne Lindsay. Copyright Anne Lindsay & Associates.

Green Beans with Sautéed Mushrooms

Serve this colourful side dish with any of the main dishes in this
cookbook.

Basic Shelf + Servings	Green beans, Mushrooms 4	
¾ lb	green beans	375 g
1 tbsp	margarine	15 mL
1	clove garlic, minced	1
	or 1/8 tsp or ½ mL garlic powder	
½ tsp	dried basil	2 mL
¼ tsp	dried rosemary	1 mL
8	medium sized mushrooms, sliced	8
dash	hot pepper sauce (optional)	dash

1. Wash green beans and trim off the ends.

2. In a saucepan of boiling water, cook beans for 6 to 8 minutes or until
    tender-crisp. Drain.

3. Meanwhile in a small saucepan, melt margarine. Add garlic, basil,
    rosemary, mushrooms and hot pepper sauce (optional). Cook over
    medium heat for 3 to 4 minutes or until mushrooms are tender.

4. Put green beans on a serving dish. Pour mushroom mixture over and
    toss to mix.

Nutrition Information per serving
• A source of fibre

Recipe from: The Lighthearted Cookbook, by Anne Lindsay, 1988. Recipe used with permission
from Anne Lindsay. Copyright Anne Lindsay & Associates.

Rice Primavera

This recipe has colour, flavour, texture, and taste! Try making this recipe with cooked pasta too. Use any extra tomatoes to make a soup.

Basic Shelf + Servings	Zucchini 6	
2 cups	water	500 mL
1 cup	rice	250 mL
2 tbsp	margarine	30 mL
¼ tsp	garlic powder	1 mL
¼ tsp	dried basil	1 mL
¼ tsp	dried oregano	1 mL
¼ cup	chopped onion	60 mL
1½ cups	sliced zucchini	375 mL
1	can (12 oz/341 mL) whole kernel corn niblets, drained and rinsed	1
1	can (10 oz/284mL) sliced mushrooms, drained and rinsed	1
1 cup	canned tomatoes	250 mL
	salt and pepper	

1. Turn on stove to high heat. Combine water and rice in a medium saucepan. Heat to boiling. Turn heat down to low, cover and simmer until rice is tender. This will take about 20 minutes and all the water will be absorbed.

2. While rice is cooking, turn on another burner to medium heat. Melt margarine in a large frypan. Stir in garlic powder, basil and oregano. Add onion and cook until soft, about 2 to 3 minutes. Add zucchini, corn and mushrooms.

3. Cook and stir over medium heat until zucchini is tender and there is no more liquid in the bottom of the frypan. This will take about 8 to 10 minutes.

4. Add cooked rice and tomatoes. Cook and stir until thoroughly heated. Add salt and pepper to taste.

Nutrition information per serving
- Good source of: folate, magnesium
- A source of fibre

Recipe from: *The Basic Shelf Cookbook,* First Edition 1994.

Rice-Stuffed Green Peppers

Green peppers are in season in the summer, so it's a good time to make a double batch of these stuffed peppers. You can freeze the stuffed peppers, and bake them another time.

Basic Shelf + Servings	Green Peppers 6	
6	medium-sized green peppers	6
1 tbsp	margarine	15 mL
1	large onion, finely chopped	1
¼ tsp	garlic powder	1 mL
1	can (28 oz/796 mL) tomatoes	1
1 cup	water	250 mL
1 cup	rice	250 mL
2 tsp	dried oregano	10 mL
2 tsp	dried basil	10 mL
	salt and pepper	
	grated cheese (optional)	
1 cup	Homestyle Tomato Sauce with Herbs* (optional)	250 mL

*   See recipe on page 22.

1. Cut a thin slice off the tops of the peppers. Carefully remove and discard the seeds and white inner ribs. Save the tops and add them to a soup or salad.

2. Cook the peppers in a medium saucepan or boiling water for 5 minutes. Drain. Place peppers upright in a small baking dish.

3. Turn on stove to medium heat. Melt margarine in a large frypan. Add onion and garlic powder. Cook until onion is soft, about 3 to 5 minutes.

4. Next, stir in tomatoes, water, rice, oregano and basil. Add salt and pepper to taste. Heat to boiling, Turn heat to low, cover and simmer until rice is tender, about 20 minutes.

...continues

Rice-Stuffed Green Peppers, continued

5. Turn on oven to 350°F (180°C).

6. Spoon rice mixture into the peppers. Bake stuffed peppers for 30 minutes or until the peppers are tender. If you like, put some grated cheese on top and continue baking until the cheese is melted.

7. Serve with hot Homestyle Tomato Sauce with Herbs (optional).

Nutrition information per serving
*   Excellent source of: vitamin C
*   Good source of: thiamine, folate, vitamin E, iron, magnesium
*   High in fibre

Recipe from: *The Basic Shelf Cookbook,* First Edition 1994.

Rice, Onion and Mushroom Pilaf

Try barley instead of rice in this recipe for a change.

Basic Shelf + Servings	Nothing to Add 4	
1 tbsp	margarine	15 mL
½ cup	finely chopped onion	125 mL
1 cup	rice	250 mL
2 cups	hot water	500 mL
1	can (10 oz/241 mL) sliced mushrooms, drained and rinsed	1
2 tsp	dried parsley	10 mL
1	chicken or beef bouillon cube	1
	salt and pepper	

1. Turn on stove to medium heat. Melt margarine in a medium saucepan. Add onion and cook until soft, about 3 to 5 minutes.

2. Stir in rice, water, mushrooms, parsley and bouillon cube. Add salt and pepper to taste. Heat until boiling. Turn heat to low, cover, and simmer until rice is tender. This will take about 20 to 25 minutes and all the water will be absorbed.

Nutrition information per serving
• A source of fibre

Recipe from: *The Basic Shelf Cookbook*, First Edition 1994.

Notes

Desserts and Baked Treats

Peach Crumble

This recipe tastes good with canned pineapple or canned fruit cocktail too. Use 2 cups (500 mL) of fresh peaches, apples or pears when they are in season.

Basic Shelf + Servings	Nothing to Add 6	
1	can (28 oz/796 mL) peach halves, drained and sliced	1 1
2 tbsp	sugar*	30 mL
¼ tsp	ground cinnamon	1 mL
1¼ cups	whole wheat flour	300 mL
1¼ cups	rolled oats	300 mL
⅔ cup	lightly packed brown sugar	150 mL
⅔ cup	margarine	150 mL

*   Add more or less sugar according to your taste.

1. Put peaches, sugar and cinnamon into a medium bowl. Stir together. Set aside.

2. Put flour, oats and brown sugar in a large bowl. Use a pastry blender or 2 knives to cut margarine into the mixture. Keep cutting until the mixture looks like crumbs. Divide oat mixture in half.

3. Turn oven on to 350°F (180°C).

4. Put one half of the oat mixture into an 8x8x2-inch (2L) baking pan. Spoon peach mixture over oat mixture base. Sprinkle remaining oat mixture on top.

5. Bake in oven until hot and browned on top, about 45 to 50 minutes.

Nutrition information per serving
• Excellent source of: vitamin A, vitamin D, magnesium
• Good source of: thiamine, niacin, iron, zinc
• Very high in fibre

Recipe from: *The Basic Shelf Cookbook*, First Edition 1994.

Creamy Rice Pudding

A delicious way to use leftover cooked rice. Add more raisins if you like.

Basic Shelf + Servings	Nothing to Add 4	
2 cups	cooked rice*	500 mL
1½ cups	water	375 mL
1 cup	skim milk powder**	250 mL
¼ cup	sugar	60 mL
¼ cup	raisins	60 mL
½ tsp	ground cinnamon	2 mL
¼ tsp	salt	1 mL
1½ tsp	vanilla extract	7 mL
	ground cinnamon - for sprinkling	

*   If you don't have 2 cups (500 mL) of leftover cooked rice, follow these directions:

Put 1 cup (250 mL) uncooked rice and 2 cups (500 mL) water into a medium saucepan. Turn on stove to high and heat to boiling. Turn heat to low, cover and simmer until rice is tender. This will take about 20 minutes and all the water will be absorbed.

** Do not use fluid milk.

1.   Put rice, water, skim milk powder, sugar, raisins, cinnamon and salt into a medium saucepan. Mix well.

2.   Turn stove on to low heat. Cook and stir until pudding is creamy. This will take about 20 minutes.

3.   Stir in vanilla extract. Sprinkle with extra cinnamon. Serve warm.

Nutrition information per serving
• Excellent source of: riboflavin, vitamin B_{12}, vitamin D, calcium
• Good source of: vitamin A, magnesium, zinc

Recipe from: *The Basic Shelf Cookbook,* First Edition 1994.

Carrot Cake

This is a large cake, perfect for special occasions. Buy the nuts from the bulk store. Any nut will work – walnuts, almonds or even pecans.

Basic Shelf + Servings	Eggs, Nuts (optional) 24	
2 cups	all purpose flour	500 mL
1¾ cups	sugar	425 mL
2 tsp	baking powder	10 mL
1 tsp	baking soda	5 mL
I tsp	ground cinnamon	5 mL
4	eggs	4
1 cup	vegetable oil*	250 mL
1 tsp	vanilla extract	5 mL
2 cups	grated carrots	500 mL
½ cup	raisins	125 mL
½ cup	chopped nuts (optional)	125 mL

*   To make this recipe lower in fat, you can use ½ cup (125 mL) vegetable oil plus ½ cup (125 mL) of either applesauce or plain yogurt instead.

1.   Turn on oven to 350°F (180°C).

2.   Mix flour, sugar, baking powder, baking soda and cinnamon in a large bowl. Set aside.

3.   Mix eggs, oil and vanilla extract in a medium bowl. Stir in grated carrots and raisins.

4.   Add carrot mixture to the dry ingredients. Mix well. Stir in nuts, if desired.

5.   Grease a 13x9x2-inch (3.5L) baking pan. Spread batter into pan.

6.   Bake on middle shelf of oven about 45 to 50 minutes. To see if the cake is baked, put a small knife into the middle of it. If the knife comes out clean, the cake is done.

7.   When cake is done remove from oven and let stand at least 10 minutes before cutting it or taking it out of the pan.

Nutrition information per serving
• Good source of: vitamin A, vitamin E

Recipe from: *The Basic Shelf Cookbook*, First Edition 1994.

Oatmeal Banana Bread

Try a slice with peanut butter and a glass of milk for breakfast or snack.

Basic Shelf + Yield	Banana, Eggs 1 Loaf (12 slices)	
2 cups	Baking Mix*	500 mL
1¼ cups	rolled oats	300 mL
2	medium bananas	2
¼ cup	water	60 mL
¼ cup	margarine	60 mL
½ cup	sugar	125 mL
2	eggs	2

* See recipe on page 21.

1. Turn on oven to 350°F (180°C). Mix Baking Mix and oats in a medium bowl. Set aside.

2. Mash bananas in a small bowl. Add water and mix. Set aside.

3. Beat margarine and sugar together in a large bowl. Beat until light and fluffy. Then beat in eggs one at a time.

4. Add dry ingredients and banana mixture to the egg mixture. Stir until just blended. Do not over mix.

5. Lightly grease a 9x5x3-inch (2 L) loaf pan. Spread batter into the loaf pan. Bake on the middle shelf of the oven for about 50 to 60 minutes. To see if the loaf is baked, put a small knife into the middle of it. If the knife comes out clean, the loaf is done.

6. Take the loaf out of the oven and cool in pan 10 minutes. Then take the loaf out of the pan.

Nutrition information per slice
• Good source of: thiamine, vitamin D
• A source of fibre

Recipe from: *The Basic Shelf Cookbook,* First Edition 1994.

Zucchini Bread

For a change, try making this with grated carrots. It is just as delicious!

Basic Shelf + Yield	Eggs, Zucchini 1 loaf (12 slices)	
1 cup	all purpose flour	250 mL
½ cup	whole wheat flour	125 mL
½ to 1 tsp	ground cinnamon	2 to 5 mL
½ tsp	baking powder	2 mL
½ tsp	baking soda	2 mL
2	eggs	2
¼ cup	sugar	60 mL
¼ cup	lightly packed brown sugar	60 mL
½ cup	vegetable oil*	125 mL
1 ⅔ cups	grated unpeeled zucchini or grated carrot	400 mL
¼ cup	raisins (optional)	60 mL

* To make this recipe lower in fat, you could use ¼ cup vegetable oil plus ¼ cup (60 mL) of either applesauce or plain yogurt instead.

1. Turn oven on to 350°F (180°C). Mix all purpose flour, whole wheat flour, cinnamon, baking powder and baking soda in a small bowl. Set aside.

2. Beat eggs in a large bowl. Stir in sugar, brown sugar and oil. Mix well.

3. Add zucchini and raisins, if desired. Mix well.

4. Add dry ingredients to the egg mixture in the large bowl. Stir until blended.

5. Lightly grease a 9x5x3-inch (2 L) loaf pan.

6. Spread batter into loaf pan. Bake on the middle shelf of the oven for about 50 to 60 minutes. To see if the loaf is baked, stick a small knife in to the middle of it. If the knife comes out clean, the loaf is done.

7. Take the loaf out of the oven and cool in the pan for about 10 minutes. Then take the loaf out of the pan.

Nutrition information per slice
• Good source of: vitamin E

Recipe from: *The Basic Shelf Cookbook*, First Edition 1994.

Banana Muffins

A perfect and delicious way to use up ripe bananas!

Basic Shelf + Yield	Bananas and Egg 12 Muffins	
½ cup	all purpose flour	125 mL
½ cup	whole wheat flour	125 mL
2 ½ tsp	baking powder	12 mL
¼ tsp	baking soda	1 mL
¾ cup	rolled oats	175 mL
½ cup	sugar	125 mL
¼ cup	lightly packed brown sugar	60 mL
½ cup	raisins (optional)	125 mL
2	medium, ripe bananas	2
1	egg	1
½ cup	milk*	125 mL
3 tbsp	margarine, melted	45 mL

*   Use fluid milk or make enough from skim milk powder.

1. Put the all purpose flour, whole wheat flour, baking powder and baking soda in a large bowl. Stir in oats, sugar, brown sugar and raisins, if desired. Set aside.

2. Mash bananas in a medium bowl. Add egg, milk and melted margarine. Mix well.

3. Stir banana mixture into the dry ingredients. Stir just until blended. Do not over mix.

4. Turn on oven to 375°F (190°C). Lightly grease 12 large muffin cups in a muffin tin. Put the muffin batter into the muffin cups, about ⅔ full.

5. Bake in oven until tops are firm when lightly touched with your finger, about 18 to 20 minutes.

6. Remove muffins from the muffin tin and cool.

Nutrition information per muffin
• A source of fibre

Recipe from: *The Basic Shelf Cookbook,* First Edition 1994.

Oatmeal Raisin Cookies

This makes a big batch. Freeze extra cookies.

Basic Shelf + Yield	Egg 24 cookies	
1¾ cups	rolled oats	425 mL
½ cup	whole wheat flour	125 mL
1 tsp	ground cinnamon	5 mL
½ tsp	baking soda	2 mL
⅓ cup	margarine	75 mL
¾ cup	lightly packed brown sugar	175 mL
1	egg	1
1 tsp	vanilla extract	5 mL
½	cup raisins	125 mL
¼ cup	water	60 mL

1. Turn on oven to 350°F (180°C). Lightly grease a baking sheet.

2. Mix oats, flour, cinnamon and baking soda in a medium bowl. Set aside.

3. Put margarine in a large bowl. Mash it with the back of spoon to soften it. Add sugar and beat well.

4. Add egg and mix well. Stir in vanilla extract. Add dry ingredients. Mix well. Stir in raisins and water.

5. Drop 12 teaspoonfuls of cookie dough onto the baking sheet, and press each one down slightly. Use about half the batter. Bake until golden brown around the edges. This will take 12 to 15 minutes. If you like your cookies crisper, bake them a few minutes longer.

6. Lift baked cookies off the baking sheet and cool. Repeat Step 5 until all the cookies are baked. Keep any extra cookies in the freezer for 4 months.

Nutrition information per cookie
• Source of: thiamine, vitamin D, magnesium

Recipe from: *The Basic Shelf Cookbook,* First Edition 1994.

Peanutty Peanut Butter Cookies

A very popular cookie! If you like your cookies firm and crisp, bake them a little longer.

Basic Shelf + **Yield**	**Eggs** **36 cookies**	
1 cup	all purpose flour	250 mL
½ cup	rolled oats	125 mL
1 ½ tsp	baking powder	7 mL
½ tsp	salt	2 mL
1 cup	peanut butter	250 mL
½ cup	margarine	125 mL
⅓ cup	sugar	75 mL
1 cup	lightly packed brown sugar	250 mL
1 tsp	vanilla extract	5 mL
2	eggs	2

1. Turn on oven to 350°F (180°C).

2. Mix flour, oats, baking powder and salt in a small bowl. Set aside.

3. Beat peanut butter and margarine together in a large bowl.

4. Stir in sugar, brown sugar and vanilla extract. Mix well.

5. Add eggs, one at a time. Mix well.

6. Stir in dry ingredients. Mix well.

7. Drop about 12 spoonfuls of cookie dough onto ungreased baking sheet. Use about one third of the batter. Bake until golden brown. This will take 10 to 15 minutes.

8. Lift baked cookies off the baking sheet and cool. Repeat Step 7 until all the cookies are baked. Keep any extra cookies in the freezer for 4 months.

Nutrition information per cookie
• Source of: niacin, folate, vitamin D, vitamin E, magnesium

Recipe from: *The Basic Shelf Cookbook*, First Edition 1994.

Date Squares

A nice sweet treat!

Basic Shelf + Yield	Dates 25 squares	
2 cups	packed, chopped, pitted dates	500 mL
1 cup	water	250 mL
1 ¼ cups	all purpose flour	300 mL
1 tsp	baking powder	5 mL
½ tsp	baking soda	2 mL
½ tsp	salt	2 mL
¾ cup	margarine	175 mL
1¼ cups	rolled oats	300 mL
¾ cup	lightly packed brown sugar	175 mL

1. Turn on oven to 350°F (180°C). Lightly grease an 8x8x2inch (2 L) baking pan.

2. Turn stove on medium heat. Put dates and water in a small saucepan. Heat to boiling. Then turn heat to low. Simmer uncovered, until mixture is as thick as jam. This will take about 10 minutes.

3. Put flour, baking powder, baking soda and salt in a large bowl. Mix.

4. Use a pastry blender or two knives to cut in margarine. Keep cutting until mixture is crumbly. Stir in oats and sugar.

5. Press half the crumb mixture into the bottom of the pan. Spread date mixture evenly over crumb mixture. Sprinkle remaining crumbs over top, pressing the crumbs lightly into the date mixture.

6. Bake in oven about 25 minutes until lightly browned. Cool in pan, then cut into squares.

Nutrition information per square
- Good source of: vitamin D
- A source of fibre

Recipe from: *The Basic Shelf Cookbook*, First Edition 1994.

Notes

Notes

Notes

Notes